THE
CITRUS
COOKBOOK

THE CITRUS COOKBOOK

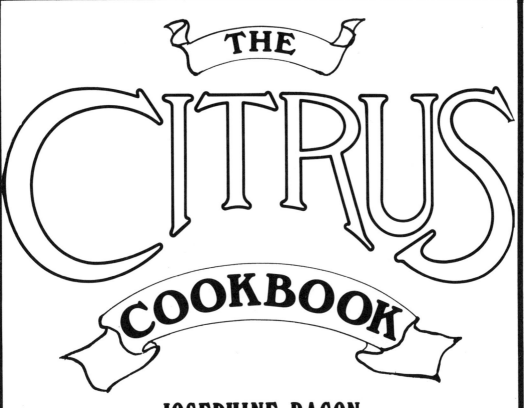

JOSEPHINE BACON

Illustrations by Nancy Simonds

THE HARVARD COMMON PRESS
Harvard and Boston, Massachusetts

The Harvard Common Press
535 Albany Street
Boston, Massachusetts 02118

Printed in the United States of America

Library of Congress Cataloging in Publication Data

Bacon, Josephine.
  The citrus cookbook.

  Bibliography: p.
  Includes index.
  1. Cookery (Citrus fruits)   I. Title.
TX813.C5B33 1983   641.6'435   83–10851
ISBN 0–916782–43–3
ISBN 0–916782–42–5 (pbk.)

Illustrations and cover design by Nancy Simonds

10 9 8 7 6 5 4 3 2 1

ISBN 0-916782-43-3 HC
ISBN 0-916782-42-5 PB

by mail is provided, as well as a bibliography for those who want to learn more about the history, development, and nutritional qualities of these magical fruits.

THE CITRUS COOKBOOK will bring sun into the lives of those frustrated cooks who live in regions where citrus may be the only fresh fruit available in the winter months, and will offer refreshment to any palate in the summer months when the cool taste of citrus is so welcome. Delightfully illustrated by New England artist Nancy Simonds, THE CITRUS COOKBOOK is sure to inspire any cook or epicure, whatever the season. And it's an ideal stocking-stuffer: along with the trad-itional holiday orange, why not include a copy of THE CITRUS COOKBOOK in someone's Christmas stocking?

candles and evergreen boughs, lights strung from trees and houses, and an orange or tangerine tucked in the toe of every Christmas stocking. Peeling away the fragrant skin to taste the sweet fruit inside is a pleasure unmatched this time of year, when markets are often empty of other fresh fruits. But citrus fruits ripen--brilliant orange, yellow, or green amid white blossoms and dense foliage--in the season when other flowering plants are dormant. For this magical quality as well as for their beauty and nutritional value, the "golden apples" of myth and legend have been treasured for over two thousand years.

A food writer for the past eight years, Josephine Bacon tells us in THE CITRUS COOKBOOK (Boston: Harvard Common Press, $14.95 cloth, $8.95 paper) how to brighten winter tables with fresh citrus fruits-- and how to use them in light and refreshing summer dishes as well. In her first chapter she introduces us to the complete range of citrus fruits, tracing their history and folklore from ancient Rome and the Orient to northern Europe and finally to modern-day Florida and California.

(over)

FOR IMMEDIATE RELEASE, PLEASE . . . .

CONTACT: Leslie Baker
(617) 423-5803

The Harvard Common Press

535 Albany Street, Boston, Massachusetts 02118 • (617) 423-5803

THE CITRUS COOKBOOK

by Josephine Bacon

Illustrated, 176 pages, 7¼" × 9¼"
$14.95 cloth (ISBN 0-916782-43-3)
$ 8.95 paper (ISBN 0-916782-42-5)

When the days are short
and the weather cold, we cele-
brate our faith that warmth is

Both familiar and exotic species are covered, since, as Bacon writes, "citrus growers are constantly developing new commercial varieties to tempt the shopper, and you may find that today's rarity becomes tomorrow's fad."

The rich, flavorful history of citrus is a perfect backdrop for the ten chapters that follow. Over 150 recipes, many collected during the author's residence in Israel, Cyprus, and southern California, span many cultures and more than eight centuries, and include uses for such unusual citrus fruits as the kumquat, the calamondin, and the pomelo. Along with such American favorites as Key Lime Pie and California Ambrosia, the recipes include seasonal classics--Lemon Mincemeat and No-Bake Fruitcake, for example--and national dishes such as Indonesian Fruit Salad, Guacamole, and Hot and Sour Soup. Bacon also covers techniques of candying citrus peel and drying citrus fruit (she even gives directions for making your own salt-free citrus spice), and she elucidates the art of making preserves--marmalades,

To Bruce Johnson, who made it all possible

CONTENTS

ACKNOWLEDGMENTS

I would like to thank the following people for their help and encouragement, and above all, their patience with my endless questions: Lewis Robison, Editor, California Citrograph; Melissa Arnold, Council of California Growers; Professor Robert Soost, University of California, Riverside; Dr. Randy Keim, South Coast Field Station, Santa Ana, California; Cliff Wurfel, Special Collections Librarian, University of California at Riverside; and Pat Sawyer and Peggy Winter, California Rare Fruit Growers Association.

INTRODUCTION

Glorious, golden citrus fruits, set off against lush green foliage, have been cultivated as much for their beauty as for their delicious flavor and nutritional properties and the fragrance of their blossoms. Citrus is in full fruit and bloom, moreover, in the bleakest season of the year, when other flowering plants are leafless and dormant. Some citrus varieties—the citron, for instance—bear fruit and blossoms simultaneously, and will do so almost year-round.

These magical qualities have stimulated the cultivation and spread of citrus fruits since ancient times. Citrus varieties were among the earliest fruits to be imported to the Western world, and they became the first major crop to be cultivated away from their native soil.

They were also the first plants to be grown in a totally hostile climate. The orangeries, conservatories, and other sheltered environments originally devised to protect these beautiful trees from the ravages of a northern winter eventually provided the means to cultivate other useful tropical plants.

The technology originally developed so the rich could grow oranges and lemons in their own gardens led not merely to the production of other unseasonable fruits and flowers for the delectation of the wealthy, but to the transplanting of valuable cash crops from one part of the world to another. Eventually, all kinds of edible and useful plants became available for consumption worldwide. The techniques first used for transporting and transplanting citrus fruits were used to bring rubber plants from the Brazilian jungle to Malaya, coffee from

Ethiopia to South America, and cocoa beans from Mexico to West Africa, thus changing the face of world agriculture.

Strangely, citrus fruit production is greatest outside the regions where the plants grow wild. The main areas of citrus cultivation today are the United States, southern Europe (Spain, Italy, Greece), North Africa, the Middle East, Australia, and South Africa. Of these, only Australia has native citrus varieties, but they are not suitable for commercial cultivation.

Citrus fruits have played key roles in both Eastern and Western cultures. They have become religious and folkloric symbols of wealth, happiness, and fertility. Their beauty has been extolled by great writers and depicted by famous painters. They are the "golden apples" of myth and legend.

The discovery of the nutritional value of citrus fruits has brought about the mass cultivation of oranges, lemons, limes, grapefruit, and tangerines. Other citrus plants are grown for the fragrance of the fruit (the citron) or the blossom (the bergamot orange). The essential oils in citrus rind are used in perfumery and polishes.

There are so many aspects to the story of citrus fruits and their cultivation that it would be impossible to cover them all in the space available here. If you want to know more about citrus than you can find in this book, consult the bibliography for guidance in further reading.

ABOUT THE RECIPES Since citrus fruits have become an integral part of the human diet, both in and out of the citrus-growing regions, the recipes in this book are drawn from every corner of the world. I have included, besides the classic citrus recipes, as many national dishes as I am aware of. I have specified the origin of a recipe where it may be of particular interest.

Since I am not fond of overelaborate creations, most of the dishes are, I hope, simple and fairly quick to prepare. The only exceptions are the candied fruits, which take time and trouble. But candying is more of a hobby than a culinary necessity, and there is no way to speed up the process. Nor have I wasted valuable space by explaining how to fashion citrus fruit into flower shapes, baskets, and so on. For those who are interested, much literature on this subject is available for free from citrus marketing organizations.

Because people who grow the more unusual varieties of citrus in their gardens or indoors are continually asking me about ways to use them, I have included hard-to-find recipes for these unusual fruits. My apologies to those who cannot lay hands on a citron or a calamondin, and who will thus find these recipes of little use. But because citrus growers are constantly developing new commercial varieties to tempt the shopper, you may find that today's rarity becomes tomorrow's new fad. The pomelo, for instance, has become a popular fruit again in northern Europe since Agrexco, the Israeli citrus marketing board, began promoting it. So do not fret, your supply of citrons and calamondins may be arriving in the corner store tomorrow!

I have included recipes using citrus products, such as orange flower water and candied peels, most of which are imported. Orange flower water is produced mainly in France and Lebanon, and candied peel is imported from South Africa, Australia, and South America. These products are easily available at good delicatessens and gourmet food shops, and are sometimes to be found in farmers' markets and even supermarkets, particularly around Christmastime.

I have tried to avoid the obvious, so I make no reference to the various juicers, squeezers, graters, and other gadgets that the reader can use or not, as he or she prefers. I am told that the best French chefs use nothing but their bare hands to squeeze oranges and lemons. My own grip is not firm enough, so I use a squeezer.

All of the recipes calling for citrus juice have been written with the fresh-squeezed variety in mind. Even food scientists are forced to admit that they are unable to reproduce the true citrus flavor in reconstituted and preserved juices. This is particularly true in the case of lime juice, which has a fragrance all its own. Furthermore, "pure" canned, freeze-dried, or concentrated citrus juice—even if it has added vitamin C—lacks the nutrients and trace minerals of fresh citrus. You can use preserved juice if you like, but there is no real substitute for the fresh fruit.

When you squeeze your own juice, likewise, you should use it immediately if you want to derive maximum nutritional benefit from it. Because vitamin C is a very volatile substance, most of this nutrient will be lost if you leave the juice overnight, even if you cover it. You can freeze citrus juice, but it will lose much of its nutritional value, just as the commercially-frozen product does.

Many of the recipes call for the fresh rind or peel of citrus fruits. Although it is supposed to be perfectly safe to eat dyed citrus peel, it is not recommended that you do so. Though Florida permits growers to dye their products, California, Arizona, and Texas do not, so you are absolutely safe with western citrus. There is no need to avoid citrus whose peel has a greenish tinge; regreening, as it is called, actually occurs after the peel has first turned orange. It does not affect the flavor of the fruit, and the peel is perfectly safe to eat (unlike green potato skins, which are poisonous). Grated peel, fresh or not, contains no vitamin C, since this important nutrient is destroyed even by cutting.

A word about seasoning. I have not specified "freshly ground" each time I mention pepper, but since all spices lose their flavor quickly once ground, it is always best to grind them just before using.

DEFINITIONS   The terms for parts of citrus fruits are variously applied. Those used in this book are defined as follows:

Rind. The colored skin of the fruit, known scientifically as the *flavedo.*

Peel. The whole of the skin, composed of the rind and the pith attached to it.

Pith. The white part of the skin attached to the colored rind.

Pulp. The flesh of the fruit.

Membrane. The white connective tissue joining the pulp to the peel.

Skin. The thin, transparent layer covering the segments of the fruit. Grapefruit and pomelos have tough skins which usually need to be removed for cooking.

Segment. One of the sections into which most citrus fruits are naturally divided. Oranges, grapefruit, tangerines, and pomelos all have between ten and twelve segments.

Except where specified otherwise, all recipe quantities are for average-sized fruit.

EQUIVALENTS

1 medium orange gives ⅓ cup juice.

3 medium oranges give 1 cup juice.

1 medium orange gives 3 teaspoons grated peel.

1 medium lemon gives 3 tablespoons juice.

6 medium lemons give 1 cup juice.

1 medium lemon gives 2 teaspoons grated peel.

1 medium grapefruit gives 12 tablespoons (⅔ cup) juice.

1 medium lime or calamondin gives 2 tablespoons juice.

1 medium lime or calamondin gives 1½ teaspoons grated peel.

1 medium mandarin or tangelo gives ½ cup juice.

1 medium mandarin or tangelo gives 3 teaspoons grated peel.

1 kumquat gives 1 teaspoon puréed or chopped fruit.

1 pound kumquats gives 3 cups purée.

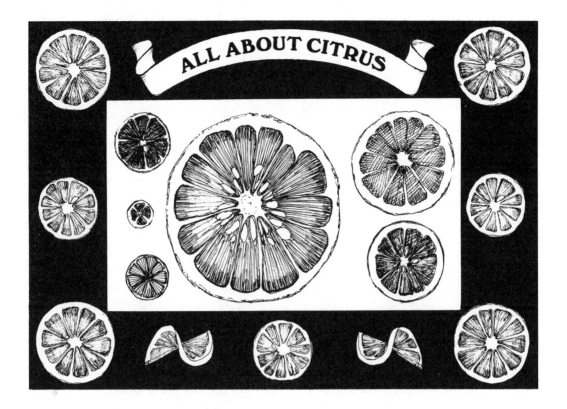

Citrus has been cultivated for so long, that for most species the exact country of origin cannot be determined. Citrus belongs to a family of plants called Rutaceae. All the plants of this family grow in the tropics or subtropics, in those areas of the world watered by the heavy summer rainfall known as the monsoon. Relatives of the orange and lemon can be found in northwestern Africa and in Australia. Although some fruits of the family Rutaceae are inedible, none are poisonous.

Citrus plants vary in their ability to withstand extremes of temperature. Those that are most susceptible to cold are believed to have originated in southern India, the East Indies, the Malay Archipelago, and the Arabian peninsula; they include the citron, pomelo, and lime. Other citruses, notably the orange and lemon, are hardier, and even require some degree of cold for the fruit to set. These species are believed to have originated on the lower slopes of the Himalayas, in India and China. Today citrus is grown even in cold climates, where it is

Orange branch with blossoms

planted indoors and taken outside on the warmest days of summer. Even where citrus is cultivated commercially, if the winter threatens to be severe heaters are brought into the orchards to warm the fruit on the coldest nights.

The hardiest member of the citrus family is the trifoliate orange, *Poncirus trifoliata*. This orange is believed to be a forerunner of other citrus varieties. It has two characteristics that make it unique among citrus plants: the leaves grow in groups of three (hence the name), and it is deciduous; all other citrus plants are evergreens with paired leaves. The trifoliate orange is hardly edible: it is dry and very sour, contains lots of seeds, and is covered with hairs. Yet when it is crossed with other, less hardy, citrus varieties, the resulting fruit is tasty as well as cold-resistant. Because of its hardiness, the trifoliate orange is often used as a rootstock. Because citrus is very susceptible to a fungus invasion of its roots, called root rot, a less resistant citrus variety is usually grafted onto the rootstock of a hardy tree, such as the trifoliate orange or the citrange, which is a cross between a trifoliate orange and a sweet orange. The plants are easy to graft, fortunately, and also crossbreed with great ease, as we shall see when we examine different citrus varieties.

Several varieties of orange, including the trifoliate orange, grow wild in China and probably originated there. So it should not be surprising that China is the source of the first written reference to citrus. *Shu-king* ("The book of history"), a collection of documents written between the twenty-fourth and eighth centuries B.C. and believed to have been collected by Confucius, contains lists of plants that include *kü* ("orange") and *yu* ("pomelo"). A poem called *Li Sao* ("Falling into trouble"), written in 314 B.C. by Ch'u Yüan, mentions the "crooked" *chih*—the trifoliate orange—and says that birds are fond of making their nests in its branches. The *kan* ("mandarin orange") was first written about in the third century A.D., at about the same time citrus was first mentioned in Roman literature.

The first citrus fruit introduced to the western world was the citron, today the least-known of the cultivated citrus fruits. It probably originated on the Arabian peninsula and was brought westward to Assyria and Persia. The ancient Hebrews, who had much contact with the Assyrians and Persians, introduced the citron to Palestine. It is the only citrus mentioned in the Bible.

The Roman author Theophrastus described the citron in 310 B.C. There is some disagreement about whether the Romans later discovered other citrus species. Representations of what appear to be oranges and lemons, as well as clearly identifiable citrons, have been found in Roman mosaics; but if oranges and lemons were introduced into Europe in the second and third centuries, as some authorities claim, they must have been rare fruits whose need for constant warmth made them difficult to cultivate even in the warmest parts of Italy. Nonetheless, citrons, if not oranges and lemons, flourished in the gardens and orangeries of the wealthy, and the trees probably grew untended after the villas were destroyed by successive invasions in the fourth century A.D. The fruits appear to have disappeared from Europe subsequently, probably after a few cold winters. Even in the wild, whole regions have been denuded of citrus by freak bad weather.

The Arabs were responsible for the spread of the bitter or sour orange. Alleged to have been brought from India in the tenth century, it was planted in Oman on the Arabian peninsula. The Arabs carried the bitter orange, and later the lemon, to all the lands they conquered, from Iraq in the east to Spain in the west. The lemon may have been cultivated by the Nabateans, a people who lived in the area covered by present-day Jordan and Iraq; it was also known to the Egyptians before the Islamic conquest. It was through the Arabs, however, that citrus fruits were introduced into northern Europe.

The crusaders first encountered citrons, bitter oranges, lemons, and limes in Syria and Palestine. The pomelo was also growing in Palestine during the Crusades, according to literature of the period.

The last major variety of citrus fruit to reach Europe was the sweet orange, which was brought from India by Portuguese explorers after they discovered the sea route from India around the Cape of Good Hope in the late fifteenth century.

Just as the Arabs spread citrus through the Islamic world, so the Spanish and Portuguese took the fruits with them on their conquests. Strangely, the actual date on which the sweet orange reached the American mainland has been recorded. It was July 12, 1518, when Juan de Grijalva landed at Tonala in the Mexican province of Vera Cruz and planted seeds brought from Cuba, whence he returned on July 20.

Thenceforth, the explorers took citrus to plant wherever they went in the new territories. The orange was introduced into Australia in 1788 by colonists of the British First Fleet under Captain Arthur Phillip, the seedlings having been bought on the way in Rio de Janeiro. The early colonists could hardly have suspected that Australia already had its own *Microcitrus australiensis* and other small citrus fruits.

Today, citrus plants are grown commercially wherever the winter climate is frost-free, and where it is not the plants are cultivated indoors as ornamentals. Thanks to cold storage and other conservation methods, there is no country in the world where fresh citrus fruits are not known and enjoyed.

THE CITRON

And ye shall take you on the first day the boughs of goodly trees . . . and ye shall rejoice before the Lord your God seven days.

Lev. 23:40

The citron (*Citrus medica*) is today the rarest and least known of citrus fruit. Yet it was the first citrus to be brought to the Western world, arriving around 500 B.C. The Greeks called the citron "cedar-apple" (*kedromelon*) because some forms resembled the cedar cone. They associated it with the mythical golden apples that grew in the garden of Hesperides.

The Romans knew the citron as "the Median apple" (*malum medicum*), because it had been introduced to the Western world from Media, in present-day Iran. Later they adopted the name *citreum* from the Greek *kitrion*. Both these names were originally applied to a certain type of cedar tree whose wood was made into tables. So the citron—and eventually the whole genus to which it belongs—got its name through confusion with a totally unrelated plant. To add to the mix-up, the type of pumpkin native to Europe and known in modern French as *citrouille* was also known to the Romans as *citreum*. Though the Romans used the pumpkin extensively in cooking, there is no genuine evidence that they ever used the citron for culinary purposes. The only Roman recipe books in existence include recipes in which *citreum* has been translated as "citron," but the reference is in fact to a pumpkin. The Romans did use the citron, however, as a medicine and as an insect repellant, and they believed it to be an antidote to poison.

Etrog citron

For a long time botanists thought the citron had originated in India, since citron trees had been found growing wild on the lower slopes of the Himalayas, in the state of Sikkim. Today, however, it is believed the citron originated in quite a different part of the world, the Arabian peninsula. There, in the fertile and well-watered mountainous regions of Hadramaut and Oman, nineteenth-century explorers found many wild varieties of cultivated fruits, including both the fig and the citron. This would explain how the fruit appears to have been introduced more or less simultaneously into Africa (Egypt), central Asia (India), and the Middle East, since the Arabian peninsula is equidistant from all three.

The citron tree is very striking, bearing fruits and flowers simultaneously almost the whole year around. Due to the abundance of its large green and yellow fruits, it has became a fertility symbol in many cultures. The fruit vary considerably in size and shape; in most of the dozen varieties they are about twice the size of a lemon. Some resemble squashes and some melons, and others are the shape and size of footballs. The football-shaped varieties are often deeply furrowed, like the cedar cone to which the species owes it name.

The Etrog variety of citron, which looks like a large, knobby lemon, is used ritually by Jews in the festival of Tabernacles. It is supposed to be the "fruit of the goodly tree" referred to in Leviticus. In order for the Etrog to be kosher for the ceremony, it must come from a tree that has not been grafted onto other rootstock. Traditionally it should have on the end opposite the stem a "nipple" (*pitma*)—actually an atro-

Etrog citron with section

Fingered citron

phied flower bud—but this is not essential. Grown mainly in Israel and Morocco and exported at a handsome price to Jewish communities all over the world, today's Etrog citrons usually lack the nipple, which is an aberration difficult to reproduce on a commercial scale.

Christopher Columbus brought citrons with him to the New World, and by 1525 they were reported by British settlers to be growing wild in St. Augustine, Florida. Though they grow well in Florida, California, and even Louisiana and Mississippi, citrons are not a commercial crop in the United States. The only commercial plantings in the Americas today are in Cuba, where the fruit is known as the Cuban shaddock, and Puerto Rico, which exports the brined peel to the United States to be made into the finest candied citrus peel available— thick, fragrant, and with an attractive green color. The Diamante citron is grown in Italy for the fragrant oils in the rind, which are used in the perfume industry. Other citron-growing countries are the Greek Isles, (especially Corfu), southwestern France, and Corsica. The Corsicans make a citron-flavored liqueur called *cédratine*.

The strangest-looking member of the entire citrus family is the Fingered citron (*Citrus medica var. sarcodactylis*), a citron variety that looks a little like a miniature bunch of bananas. It is colored green or deep yellow, and its externally divided segments have little or no pulp. The fingered citron has been greatly prized by the Chinese and Japanese, who call it the Hand of Buddha and use it as a room deodorizer and symbol of fertility. Cultivation is waning however, as the citrus-growing areas in both countries are limited, and suitable land is being devoted more and more to edible citrus varieties. For this reason the pomelo has taken the place of the citron in Chinese new year celebrations.

The decline in the popularity of the citron began about two hundred years ago, with the introduction of the sweet orange and other sweet citrus varieties into Europe and the start of large-scale planting and consumption of citrus. The citron is not easy to eat raw; the very thick skin is as bitter as grapefruit skin. The citron has little pulp, and what it has is rather dry and contains a large number of seeds. The pulp will not separate easily from the skin and must be scraped away.

Citrons have become unpopular with commercial growers mainly because they are exceptionally sensitive to cold; for this reason they are planted at the edges of citrus orchards in the United States as "frost markers." It is also difficult to get citrons to fruit, due to their production of large quantities of infertile male flowers, and they are susceptible to root rot and other diseases. Nonetheless, it is high time citrons were promoted by nurseries as ornamentals, for their beauty as well as their rarity and historic importance.

THE LEMON, SWEET AND SOUR

I'll be with you in the squeezing of a lemon.
Oliver Goldsmith
She Stoops to Conquer, 1773

The lemon is, unquestionably, the most versatile of all the fruits of the earth. It has been cultivated for so long that wild varieties are unknown. The fruit was brought to the Mediterranean region by the Arabs, probably from the East Indies and Malaya, where the Arabs traded in spices so profitably for many centuries. Many botanists believe the lemon is actually a hybrid or mutation of the citron; nevertheless, they have classified it as a separate species with the Latin name *Citrus limon.*

The lemon did not reach the West until the twelfth century, but it quickly established itself in Palestine and Persia. Today the biggest lemon crops in the Mediterranean area are in southern Italy (mainly Sicily), Israel, Cyprus, and Spain. Columbus brought the lemon to the West Indies on his second voyage in 1493, and the seeds were introduced to Florida from Haiti in the early sixteenth century. Lemons have never been an important crop in Florida, however, although plantings were started there again in the early 1950s. Lemons prefer arid climates, since a long dry spell is needed for the fruit to set. Today, the biggest lemon crop in the world is grown in the California-Arizona sun belt.

The main commercial lemon variety grown in the United States is the Eureka. Other varieties to be found in the stores

Eureka lemon

are the Villafranca and the Lisbon lemon, which are grown mainly in Florida. The Ponderosa lemon, a large, thick-skinned variety that is a recent hybrid between a lemon and a citron, is also found in the market occasionally. More delicious than any of these is the Meyer lemon, a sweet, juicy fruit with a thin, smooth skin. Some botanists believe that the Meyer, which originated in China, is not a true lemon but a cross between a lemon and an orange. At one time, unfortunately, the Meyer carried a virus that could have damaged other citrus, so the sale of the fruit was restricted. Meyer lemons are the most popular variety for home growing in California, where a new virus-free strain has recently been developed by the University of California.

Another kind of lemon which reached the Americas early on is the rough lemon, *Citrus jambhiri*, which originated in India and was brought to Florida by Spanish settlers in the early sixteenth century. The fruit is not particularly juicy, but the trees are very attractive and are grown as ornamentals, particularly in Arizona. The great commercial importance of the rough lemon, however, is as a rootstock; most Florida oranges are grown on rough lemon rootstock. Because of their hardiness, the trees have established themselves in the wild in several parts of the world, notably along river beds in southern Africa (where the fruit is known as the Mazoe lemon for the Mazoe River in Zimbabwe) and in the Florida Keys.

The lemon tree is large and handsome. Since it can be espaliered or trimmed into a decorative hedge, it is much in demand as a yard tree in the Sun Belt. The flowers are fragrant and attractively tinged with purple. Lemons have two great advantages as a commercial crop: they can be persuaded to fruit almost year-round, and they store better than any other citrus fruit. In southern California they are harvested all year; however, the best and cheapest lemons are available from December to March.

The rind, juice, and even the pith and seeds of the lemon contain a variety of valuable ingredients. Lemon juice contains more ascorbic acid (vitamin C) than the juice of any other citrus fruit. Although some noncitrus fruits have a higher vitamin C content, they are not as easy to grow as the lemon,

Rough lemon

and their juice is more difficult to extract. Lemon juice was known to cure scurvy even in Columbus's time, though it was not until centuries later that navies and commercial shipping companies could be persuaded that the lives of sailors were valuable enough to warrant supplying their vessels with a stock of fresh citrus.

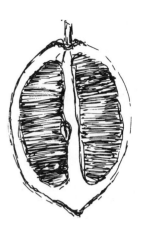

The popularity of the lemon as food is due to the combination of flavors in the juice, with sourness predominating. The lemon's sourness derives mainly from its citric acid content. The human palate can distinguish between only three flavors—sweet, salty, and sour—the rest are actually smelled rather than tasted. Sourness is therefore a keynote of good cooking. Before citrus fruits were widely known in Europe, sourness was produced from other sour fruits, all of whose juices were called *verjuice*. In northern Europe crabapple juice was used; in France and southern Europe the flavor came from sour grape juice. But these were quickly supplanted by lemon juice, which provided sourness combined with fragrance and flavor, as soon as lemons became widely available.

Citric acid, first discovered in lemon juice, is an extremely valuable industrial chemical. It is used in medicines, engraving compounds, dyes, plastics, and synthetic resins. Lately it has become a popular ingredient in detergents, though mostly for its fragrance. The oil in lemon rind is the most valuable of the citrus oils, and it is commercially extracted for use as a perfume and flavoring. (It is also used in furniture polish in the United States; however, lemon oil is actually very drying, and it is most unsuitable as a preservative for fine woods.)

In the kitchen, lemon juice is a valuable bleach and antioxidant. Added to white fruits and vegetables, such as apples, artichokes, jicama, and potato, it will prevent the cut flesh from oxidizing and turning brown. Mixed with salt, lemon juice is an excellent bleach and disinfectant; and, of course, it is absolutely safe to use on utensils that will come into contact with food. Unlike commercial bleaches such as ammonia and chloride of lime, it is nonpoisonous and leaves no aftertaste. To remove stains from any metal saucepan, boil a handful of coarse (kosher) salt with the juice of a lemon in a panful of water. Copper pans and bowls for use with food should be scoured

Mediterranean sweet lemon

only with coarse salt applied with the cut half of a lemon. Lemon will not only soften and whiten the skin safely, it is also a natural antiseptic. A chef's trick is to rub the hands with a cut lemon while slicing meat or fish, particularly shellfish. If you cut your hand while working, there is little risk of infection if your skin has been cleaned with lemon juice.

Lemon peel can be used fresh or dried as a flavoring and makes a good salt-free seasoning.

Even lemon seeds and pith are useful, since they are richer than any other citrus fruit in pectin, which is derived commercially from the pith and seeds of lemons. Instead of buying commercial pectin when making jams and jellies from low-acid fruits, such as strawberries and raspberries, try adding the pith and seeds of two lemons, wrapped in cheesecloth, when you cook the fruits and sugar. You can add the lemon pulp as well; it is also rich in pectin, and the juice it releases will improve the flavor of whatever preserve you are making.

All of the foregoing concerns the sour lemon. Less widely known is the sweet lemon, which has been classified as a separate species, *Citrus limetta*. It is also known as the limetta (*lumie* in French). There are three main kinds of sweet lemon: the Marrakesh limonette, the Mediterranean sweet limetta, and the Millsweet sweet lemon. Only the Millsweet is cultivated in the United States; it can be found in the gardens of the San Gabriel Mission near Los Angeles. But not even the Millsweet is grown commercially in this country.

Though sweet lemons are very juicy and are indistinguishable from sour lemons in appearance, they lack the high acid content of the sour variety. Consequently, most experts agree, their flavor is insipid. They make delicious lemonade, however, without the addition of sugar.

THE BITTER ORANGE

*Fine oranges, sauce for your veal
Are charming when squeez'd in a pot of brown ale.*
                                        Jonathan Swift

Bitter oranges, which are sometimes also known as sour oranges, bigarades, and Seville oranges, are the most beautiful of citrus trees. They are the only citrus grown exclusively for the perfume in their fruit, blossoms, and leaves. There are several varieties of bitter oranges, of which the sour orange (*Citrus aurantium*) is the most common.

Bitter oranges are believed to have originated on the southern slopes of the Himalayas, in the region now made up of northeastern India, Burma, and southwestern China. The Moors, who discovered the sour orange in India, planted the trees not only for their beauty but also for their juice, which they used much as we use the juice of the lemon—as a flavoring for food, drinks, and medicines. Like their eastern counterparts, the Moghuls, the Moors planted orange groves wherever they settled; they introduced the sour orange to Europe in the early Middle Ages. Perhaps the most famous plantations of sour oranges are in Spain, which is why the sour orange is often known as the Seville orange.

In the latter part of the eighth century the Grand Vizier, Al-Mansur, completed the Great Mosque at Corboda and the famous Patio de los Naranjos adjoining it. The colonnades of the great mosque are echoed in the lines of elegant trees, with their bare trunks, lime-washed against sunburn, topped by solid masses of the dark green foliage with which the large, fragrant white blossoms and orange fruit contrast so well. A similar orange orchard was planted in front of the great mosque, now a cathedral, in the city of Seville.

As the bitter orange spread through Europe from Spain, more and more people wanted to grow it—indoors, if necessary. Thus began the building of orangeries to house these miraculous winter-fruiting trees. One of the earliest orangeries was built in 1562 by Lord Burghley, Lord Chamberlain to Queen Elizabeth I of England. Queen Henrietta Maria, wife of the ill-fated Charles I, had an "orange court" at Wimbledon, now a south London suburb. Her trees were grown in the open, but heavily sheltered from the weather. The construction of the great orange houses of Europe, elegant buildings with huge windows, began only in 1601, when the Elector Palatine of Heidelberg had the first solid structure built to house his citrus collection.

The eagerness of the rich and powerful to grow these

lovely trees stimulated a search for stronger and better glass, more effective heating systems, and still more exotic plant varieties. Eventually these technological developments were practically applied in transplanting commercially useful tropical and subtropical plants from one part of the world to another. The sour orange was one of the first citrus plants brought to the American shores. (Like the rough lemon, it now grows wild in southern Florida, where large groves of sour oranges can be found.) What started as a rich man's fancy has revolutionized world agriculture.

The country that consumes the largest quantity of sour oranges today is Great Britain. The British have a passion for marmalade made from bitter or Seville oranges; they consider the sweet orange too insipid. They also use bitter oranges in the manufacture of steak sauces, the thick brown concoctions that come out of bottles labeled "O.K." or "H.P.," which they use to disguise the taste of their food.

The bitter but fragrant oils in the peel of the oranges have long been appreciated as an addition to alcoholic beverages. The Dutch were probably first to use the bitter orange peel to flavor gin and wine; since then it has been used in many varieties of "bitters." It is also the main ingredient in orange liqueurs such as Curaçao (first made in Holland from bitter oranges imported from the island of the same name in the Dutch East Indies), Grand Marnier (made from Haitian bitter oranges), and triple sec.

Important ingredients in European cooking of the Renaissance, the grated rind and juice of bitter oranges still feature prominently in certain cuisines, notably that of Mexico, where they are used as bittersweet flavorings and in marinades for meat and fish.

Because of their strong fragrance, the blossoms of the bitter orange were favorite gifts from suitors to their loved ones in eighteenth-century France—hence the traditional bridal bouquet of orange blossoms. Today the bitter orange blossom is even more important commercially than the peel and pulp. A variety of bitter orange called a *bouquetier*, or "perfume tree," is grown for the essential oil, called neroli, that is extracted from the flowers for use in cosmetics and perfumes.

A byproduct of neroli is orange flower water, which was the principal flavoring extract before vanilla became widely known. It is still used extensively in cooking, particularly in the Middle East. *Bouquetiers* are grown mainly in France, Lebanon, Italy, Spain, Portugal, Morocco, and Paraguay.

Branch of the bitter orange

Another variety of bitter orange is the myrtle-leafed orange, better known as the Chinotto of Italy. The Chinotto probably originated in China, as its name suggests. Today it is cultivated commercially only in the Italian province of Liguria, where it is grown for its fruit, which is candied or made into preserves. Elsewhere the tree is grown as an ornamental.

Although modern botanists would put it in a category of its own, the Bergamot (*Citrus bergamia*) has been traditionally classified as a bitter orange. (It should not be confused with the North American herb known as bergamot, which was so named because its fragrance is very similar to that of the bergamot orange.) The Bergamot may be a hybrid of the bitter orange and, possibly, the lemon. Its fruit is lemon yellow, in contrast to the brilliant orange color of the true bitter orange. Bergamot oranges are cultivated almost exclusively in Calabria, the southernmost province of Italy. The oil extracted from the rinds has great commercial importance, since it is the basic constituent of eau de Cologne. Petitgrain oil, distilled from the young shoots and leaves of the tree, is used in perfumes, soaps, and cosmetics.

It is sad that the bitter orange is so rarely seen in the United States. This beautiful tree deserves to be planted more often as a shade tree and ornamental in public parks and on streets. Its hardiness makes it suitable for cultivation even outside the citrus belt, provided it is sheltered from winter frosts.

THE LIME
Bear me, Pomona! to thy citron groves
To where the lemon and the piercing lime,
With the deep orange glowing through the green
Their lighter glories blend.

James Thomson
"The Seasons: Summer," 1727

If the bitter orange has the most fragrant citrus blossoms, the lime undoubtedly has the most fragrant fruit. Both the essential oils in the rind and the flesh itself are permeated with a refreshing perfume that even the most sophisticated technology has been unsuccessful in reproducing artificially, despite many attempts.

Although limes strongly resemble lemons in appearance, degree of acidity, and even color, botanists have classified them as a different species, *Citrus aurantifolia*. But the two citrus varieties are constantly confused, so much so that it is impossible to distinguish between lemons and limes in most early references to the fruits. Apart from the botanical differences, such as size, color, and clustering of the blossoms, limes are more sensitive to the cold than lemons; they require warmth year-round. In the United States limes can be grown only in the southernmost areas of California and Florida, and large quantities must be imported from Mexico to satisfy demand. Like lemons, limes can be grouped into two subspecies, sweet and sour; all commercially cultivated varieties fall in the latter category.

Limes were brought westward with the sour orange by the Arabs, who planted sweet and sour limes in the warmest parts of the Moorish empire, in southern Iraq, in southern Persia, and in Palestine. The first Europeans to encounter the limes were the crusaders, who saw them in Palestine. Though some trees have been planted outdoors in southern Italy and Spain, limes are grown on a commercial scale only in subtropical climates in the Americas and parts of Africa. In northern Australia there is a native wild lime, the finger lime (*Microcitrus australiensis*).

Columbus included limes among the citrus fruits he brought to Hispaniola on his second voyage in 1493, and they quickly established themselves in the warm, moist climate of the Caribbean. The first Spanish settlers in Florida brought limes with them. The trees flourished in the Keys, hence the name Key lime.

Also known as the West Indian or Mexican lime, the Key lime is a smallish fruit whose rind remains greenish yellow even at maturity; the flesh is also green. The tree bears fruit almost year-round, though the biggest crop is produced in the winter. This variety, which is very similar to the sour limes grown in Egypt, Morocco, and Brazil, is the most popular commercial variety worldwide. This was the lime that the British Navy supplied its sailors as protection against scurvy and that hence earned the British the nickname limey. In fact, British ships carried lemon juice on board as an antiscorbutic long before they carried lime juice; in 1593 Sir James Lancaster distributed juice from lemons grown on the island of St. Helena to the sailors on his ship during the long voyage from India to Africa, and his contemporaries were aware that the lemon juice was responsible for the lack of scurvy among the sailors on his ship. But it was not until 200 years later, when lime juice could be imported cheaply from the British colony of Jamaica, that this antiscorbutic became regulation issue to British sailors. Although it was known even in the eighteenth century that lemon juice is more effective in combating scurvy— it is twice as rich in vitamin C as lime juice—limes, unlike lemons, did not have to be bought from the foreign (and often hostile) Mediterranean countries. The sailors drank their lime juice with the rum ration, and naval officers stood by to see that both juice and rum were drunk as soon as they were issued.

Mexican lime and Eureka lemon

The other main commercial lime variety, the Tahiti or Persian lime, was introduced to Florida from Tahiti only in the mid-nineteenth century. It has a larger fruit than the Key lime, and the rind is pale yellow at maturity. The Tahiti lime grows in the warmer parts of the Arab world and in that part of Iran that borders on the Persian Gulf. It is often used in dried form in the Middle East, where it is known in Arabic as *lamoon amani* (Oman lemon) or *numi basra* (Basra lime).

Another commercially grown variety is the Bearss lime,

often confusingly referred to as a Bearss lemon because it has a lemon yellow rind with greenish yellow flesh. In the United States, the Bearss lime is grown almost exclusively in California. It resembles the Tahiti lime, to which it is probably closely related.

The sweet lime, which grows in the same regions of the world as the sour lime, has never been held in high regard by Americans. It comes in only one variety, *Citrus limettoides*, known variously as the Indian sweet lime or the Palestine sweet lime.

The Rangpur lime, a popular houseplant and yard tree in the United States, is not really a lime at all. Although it has a lime-like fragrance, it is probably related to the mandarin, which it resembles closely in shape and color. It has a separate botanical name, *Citrus limonia.*

The Otaheite, considered a dwarf variety of the Rangpur lime, is also known as the Otaheite orange. It was introduced to Europe from Tahiti in 1813, and was brought to the United States in the 1880s, where it quickly gained popularity as a potted plant. It is well suited for indoor planting.

The Kaffir lime (*Citrus hystrix*), like the Rangpur, has a misleading name—it is neither a kaffir (South African native) nor a lime. It belongs to a citrus species known as papeda, and it is found chiefly in Ceylon and Indonesia. The fruit, which is rather dry-fleshed and bears a superficial resemblance to the rough lemon, is not eaten, but is used in washing hair and as an insect repellent. In Indonesia the leaves of the Kaffir lime are used in cooking; their flavor is similar to that of the curry leaves of Indian cuisine. Papedas are not now grown commercially, but they may eventually be cultivated as rootstocks for edible citrus.

To add to the confusion, neither the Spanish lime nor the Naranjilla (Spanish for "little orange"), two tropical fruits popular in Florida, are citrus. Both were named for their citrus-like flavor.

The fragrance of lime juice and lime rind, combined with their sour flavor and strong acidity, make them irreplaceable in cooking and perfume manufacture. But though the United States is the biggest commercial producer of limes in the world, fresh limes are not as easily available outside the areas in which they are grown as are the other commercial varieties of citrus. This is a great pity.

> *These fruits* [kumquats] *are eaten without peeling their golden coats. When preserved in honey, their flavor is still better . . . At first the people of the capital* [Btijing] *did not value them very highly, but subsequently, owing to the Empress Wen Ch'eng, the wife of the Emperor Yen-Tsung, of the Sung dynasty* (A.D. *1023–1064), having manifested a liking for the fruit, it became popular.*
>
> Chü lu (a monograph on citrus)
> Han Yen-Chih, 1178

THE KUMQUAT AND THE CALAMONDIN

The above description of the kumquat appears in the first known Chinese work on citrus fruits, and is probably based on even earlier material. The name *kumquat* is said to be a corruption of *chin kan* or *kin kan,* the Chinese and Japanese words for "golden orange." This miniature citrus fruit grows on a full-sized tree, but from time immemorial the plant has been dwarfed to produce an attractive ornamental. In ancient China an alternative name for the kumquat was *chi k'o ch'eng,* ("give guest orange"), due to the custom of presenting the dwarf trees covered in still green fruit to friends and guests. Today Florida growers do a brisk trade in dwarf kumquat trees, which are sold all over the country as ornamentals and houseplants and in citrus gift packages.

The kumquat appears to have been brought to Europe in 1846 by Robert Fortune, an Englishman, who in that year presented a specimen to the Royal Horticultural Society in London. Botanists decided to classify the kumquat separately from the genus *Citrus,* although it is obviously closely related to the true citrus. In recognition of Robert Fortune's contribution, kumquats have been given the generic name *Fortunella.*

The kumquat that Robert Fortune brought to England, and that was soon sent to Florida, was the Nagami or oval kumquat. The round-fruited Marumi was introduced into Florida from Japan in 1885, and the Meiwa and Hong Kong kumquats between 1910 and 1912. Meiwa is the juiciest and

Meiwa kumquat

Nagami kumquat and limequat

sweetest of the kumquats; the Hong Kong, which grows wild on that island, is used exclusively as an ornamental, since the seeds are so large that there is virtually no pulp.

Although kumquats can be eaten raw and are the only citrus whose skins are entirely edible, they are more often candied and made into marmalades and preserves. Kumquats are now grown in both Florida and California, and are in season from November to March.

The kumquat has often been crossed with other citrus fruits because it is so resistant to cold. Two hybrids of kumquats and limes are important. The best known of these is the Philippine lime, or calamondin (*Citrus madurensis*), which has a tart flavor and strong aroma and looks like a small mandarin. This fruit is grown throughout southeast Asia and, as its name implies, is an important crop in the Philippines, where it is squeezed directly over foods as a condiment and is used in sweet and sour sauces and refreshing drinks. Calamondins are also cultivated in Florida, mainly as houseplants and for sale to Filipino food stores. They are also called by their Filipino name, kalamansi. The kumquat has also been crossed with the Key lime to produce the limequat, a popular ornamental that produces a delicious lemon yellow fruit.

THE SWEET ORANGE

What should wt do but sing His praise, [. . .]
He hangs in shades the orange bright,
Like golden lamps in a green night

Andrew Marvell
"Bermudas," 1681

It is a mystery why the sweet orange—the pride of the citrus family—reached Europe so late, and did not become widely appreciated until long after the lemon, the sour orange, the lime, and the pomelo. It was not until 1500 A.D. at the earliest that the sweet orange came into its own.

The greatest authority on the subject, the late Shmuel Tolkowsky, asserted that the sweet orange (*Citrus sinensis*) must have been known to the Romans, but that the trees were destroyed as a consequence of the invasions of the fifth century A.D. Other historians claim the first sweet oranges were brought to Europe from India by Vasco da Gama, the Portuguese explorer, and by successive Portuguese traders. Certainly, the Portuguese wrote enthusiastically about the sweet oranges they found in southern India and Ceylon. These oranges were soon planted in Portugal, where they flourished; in many languages the word *portugal* has become synonymous with *sweet orange*.

Historians believe that sweet oranges were known in Europe prior to the sixteenth century, but that because their flesh was dry and their flavor insipid, they were considered inferior to the sour orange, whose abundant juice was so useful as a flavoring and a condiment. A clue is provided by the existence in Palestine of a semi-wild sweet orange which the Arabs call *fransawi* ("French.") This orange is inferior in quality even to the Baladi, the so-called native orange, let alone the Shamouti, the famous Jaffa orange, which is probably the sweetest and most flavorful of all orange varieties. But this may well have been the orange ordered by Louis XI of France for Saint Francis of Paula, whom King Louis invited to the French court in 1483. The king asked the governor of Provence, the French province famous for its citriculture, to send him fresh fruits for the saint, who seems to have been a vegetarian. The fruits included sweet oranges, and these may well have been the "French" oranges of Palestine.

At the end of the sixteenth century, after the Portuguese had established trading posts in southern China, it was rumored in Europe that Chinese sweet oranges surpassed even the Indian variety known as the portugal. Although the Portuguese did their best to keep China oranges for themselves, the seeds were smuggled out of Portuguese trading posts in China and were soon producing trees throughout the Mediterranean area.

The China orange was imported into Northern Europe in such quantities that it soon became a common item of trade, though it remained a luxury. Writing in 1668, Samuel Pepys claimed oranges cost sixpence a piece, the equivalent of at least two dollars in today's terms. No doubt the popularity of the fruit in seventeenth-century England was heightened by the fact that the pretty "orange wenches" were reputed to sell more than merely fruit in the streets of London. Nell Gwynne

Orange with blossom

("Sweet Nell of Old Drury") first encountered King Charles II of England while selling oranges in the pit of the Theatre Royal, Drury Lane (which is still going strong but, alas, minus orange sellers). This was yet more evidence to support the popular belief of the time that oranges and lemons were powerful aphrodisiascs—another good explanation for the bridal orange blossom bouquet and wreath.

Sweet oranges probably reached Florida in 1565, when the first Spanish settlement was established at St. Augustine. Almost simultaneously, Spanish colonists were planting sweet oranges on the islands off the Carolina and Georgia coasts. According to many accounts, the seeds of all the varieties of citrus introduced to these parts were spread by Indians, and the trees established themselves in the wild. Although the citrus groves of southern Florida were composed mainly of sour oranges, a few sweet orange trees were among them.

Yet it was not until Florida was ceded to the United States in 1821 that citrus became a commercial crop there. As transportation improved, sweet oranges were planted near to bodies of water so they could easily be shipped northward for the Christmas trade. Packed in barrels lined with Spanish moss, oranges were shipped to New York and Boston, where they fetched a handsome price. This trade was temporarily halted in 1835, when a terrible frost damaged most of the orange trees down to their roots. Although many trees recovered, the growers abandoned northern Florida and henceforth concentrated their efforts in the central and southern parts of the state, principally along the St. Johns river south of Jacksonville. The introduction of the railroads to the state provided a further boost to trade. By 1886 Florida orange exports to other states exceeded a million boxes.

The great freezes of 1894 and 1895 wrecked the entire orange industry in Florida. Groves were replanted, only to be destroyed again by the frost of 1899. Although the industry recovered, severe frosts continued to occur at about twenty-year intervals, though techniques were eventually developed to give the trees some measure of protection against the cold. But warm air from heaters and fans could reach only the smallest trees. The older trees, including sweet oranges that had been grafted

Orange branch with developing fruit

on wild sour orange rootstocks, were too large to be protected, and all of them died. That is why none of the original sweet orange plantations have been preserved.

This did not happen in California, fortunately. The Washington navel, the sweet orange tree imported from Brazil that made Riverside world-famous, still stands in the center of the city, carefully protected by iron railings. Seedlings of this variety of navel orange, which was first discovered in the state of Bahia, Brazil, and is known elsewhere as the Bahia orange, were introduced into Australia in 1824 and into Florida in 1835. In 1870 the United States Department of Agriculture obtained some of the trees and had them planted in the USDA greenhouses in Washington. They were subsequently distributed to several growers, including Mrs. Eliza Tibbets of Riverside, California, who planted a few in her yard in 1871. In 1879 her oranges were the star attraction at the Riverside Citrus Fair, where they were awarded first prize among navels. The Washington navel soon became the leading commercial orange variety in California, though its prime position has recently been supplanted by the Valencia, a late-fruiting variety that comes into its own when the season is over for other sweet oranges.

Washington navel

Citrus plantings in the West began long before Mrs. Tibbets planted her tree. The first orchards were planted by Spanish Jesuits at their Arizona missions as early as 1707. When the Franciscans, under the leadership of Father Junipero Serra, established their first California mission at San Diego in 1769, sweet orange trees were brought from Mexico and planted in the mission grounds. The first large sweet orange grove in California was planted at the San Gabriel Mission, near Los Angeles.

The first commercial grower in California was William Wolfskill, a Kentuckian who settled in Los Angeles in 1831; ten years later he decided to grow oranges for sale. He bought some sweet orange seedlings from the San Gabriel Mission and went into business. Wolfskill's neighbors mocked him for embarking on such a ridiculous and foolhardy enterprise. He had the last laugh, of course; the final crop sold in his lifetime fetched $25,000 on the tree!

More planting was stimulated by the Gold Rush, but it

Navel orange blossom

was not until the railroad finally linked California with the east in the late 1870s that the orange trade really blossomed. The first shipment of oranges from California reached St. Louis in 1877. Although the fruits were one month in transit, they arrived in good condition.

Riverside, founded only a year before Mrs. Tibbets planted her trees there, became the center of the citrus industry, although orchards were planted all over Los Angeles, Riverside, San Bernardino, and Orange counties. The Riverside growers were great innovators, creating heaters for the groves (the "smudging pot" oil heaters so common on cold nights in the citrus groves of California and Florida), crate-making machinery, and even the first individual fruit wrapper. These and other southern California growers founded the first agricultural cooperative—the California Fruit Growers Exchange, now known as Sunkist.

Another California invention, which would not have been possible without great technological advances in printing, was the orange crate label. These brilliantly colored and imaginatively designed advertisements were affixed to crates of California oranges to be shipped east, especially in the 1920s and 1930s. The golden fruits and romantic scenes depicted on the labels inspired many a shivering orange eater to leave the harsh climate of the east and try his luck in sunny California.

Today the orange crop of the United States is the biggest in the world, although there are large harvests in South Africa, Australia, and the countries of the eastern Mediterranean and North Africa. The most popular commercial varieties are seedless or almost seedless. They include various navels, the Jaffa orange or Shamouti, and the Mediterranean Sweet (known outside the United States as the Maltese Oval). Most orange-growing areas have developed their own varieties, such as the Parson Brown in Florida, the Marrs in Texas, and the Poorman in Australia—all of which are named for the growers who first produced them.

An unusual sweet orange variety is the blood orange, whose pigmentation ranges from blood-colored streaks in the pulp to a ruby coloration of the entire pulp and rind. Blood oranges are grown mainly in the Mediterranean area, especially in Spain, Malta, and Italy. The coloration seems to have

Maltese Oval

developed spontaneously in cultivated oranges, since blood oranges are unknown in the wild. Although both fresh blood oranges and their processed juice are especially popular in Germany and Scandinavia, they are disliked in the United States. Some blood oranges are grown in Florida and California, but, for some unexplained reason, they do not have the intense coloration of the European oranges.

To enhance their flavor, oranges have been crossed with tangerines and mandarins, and the resulting hybrids are known as tangors. Some tangors, such as the Temple, Murcott, and King, are popularly called oranges, but they display many characteristics of the tangerine or mandarin. This is especially true in the case of the King, which has the loose peel of the tangerine, though it lacks the tangerine's resistance to cold. Another such cross has produced the Ortanique, which is grown mainly in Spain and the West Indies.

Sweet oranges have also been crossed with the trifoliate orange; the result is called a citrange. Though some of these hybrids are inedible, they are useful as ornamentals and yard trees in areas where it is too cold in winter for other citrus fruits. Another ornamental that has little food value is the citrangequat, a cross between a citrange and the kumquat.

Blood orange

THE MANDARIN

> *The scent of tachibana flowers in May*
> *Recalls the perfumed sleeves of him who is no longer here.*
>   Izumi Shikibu, 1003

In Japanese mythology the Tachibana tangerine is the tree of life that grows in the eternal land of Shinto. A Tachibana tree guards the steps leading to the emperor's chambers, and during the Japanese new year celebration Tachibanas hang at the door of the house with a pine branch and other symbols of luck, renewal, and long life. It is believed that the two Japanese varieties of loose-skinned oranges, the Tachibana and the Mikan mandarin, were originally brought to Japan from Fukien province in China.

Both in China and Japan, these fruits have always been associated with the nobility; hence the generic name *mandarin* and its Latin equivalent, *Citrus nobilis*.

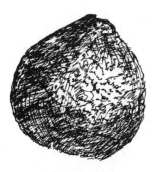

King mandarin

An easily removed peel being almost the only common quality that sets mandarins apart from other oranges, their otherwise widely differing characteristics have caused confusion in their botanical classification. The name *tangerine* has come to be applied to some varieties of these sweet oranges, particularly those belonging to the subspecies known in Latin as *Citrus reticulata*. Today the two names are used interchangeably.

These delicious fruits of the Orient, which are now overtaking oranges in popularity, did not reach Europe until 1805, when Sir Abraham Hume brought two of the plants to England from China. A loose-skinned orange of the tangerine family was already being grown in the Mediterranean basin, however, though its cultivation there began no earlier than 1800. This variety, called the Mediterranean or Willowleaf mandarin, has been given a separate Latin name, *Citrus deliciosa*.

Although the mandarin is reputed to have been introduced into Florida around 1825, the first hard evidence of mandarins in the United States is with the introduction of the Mediterranean or Willowleaf mandarin by the Italian consul in New Orleans, at some time between 1840 and 1850.

Among the most popular commercial varieties worldwide are the Satsuma, round and squat with a thick skin and pale, seedless, orange yellow flesh; the Wilkins or Wilkings, small and juicy with bright orange-red skin and lots of seeds; the Honey mandarin, with a fairly tight-fitting golden skin and honey-sweet flesh; and the Dancy, named for Colonel Dancy, a famous Florida grower who nicknamed mandarins "kid-glove oranges." Other popular varieties in the United States are the Kinnow mandarin, another tight-skinned variety, and the Kara, which fruits quite late.

Because they fruit earlier than sweet oranges, mandarins and tangerines have since their introduction been especially popular in northern Europe, where they have become almost mandatory at the Christmas table. Among the varieties most often imported into northern Europe, apart from the Satsuma, are the Naartje from South Africa, which is also sold in crystallized form, and the Clementine. The Clementine, a tangerine variety first grown in Algeria by Father Clement Rodier, is a cross between the Mediterranean tangerine and the sour or

Satsuma mandarin

bitter orange. Its skin is reddish orange with prominent oil glands, and it has few seeds. The Clementine is grown throughout the Middle East and in the United States besides in its native North Africa, and it is very popular in Europe because of its early maturity.

A hybrid as popular as the tangor is the tangelo, a cross between a tangerine and a grapefruit. The best known of these in the United States is the Minneola, a distinctive fruit with its deep orange red color and large nipple-like protrusion at the stem end. Grown in the southern California deserts, it is in season between January and March. Other tangelos, grown mainly in Florida, are the Orlando and the Seminole, both rather seedy varities; the Seminole is especially tart in flavor. The most popular tangelo that has originated outside the United States, the Ugli Fruit, is grown in Jamaica and exported to Canada and Europe. The Ugli, with its bumpy surface, lives up to its name but has a pleasant flavor.

Tangelo

And shaddock mid the garden-paths, on bough
Freshest like fairest damsel met my sight;
And to the blowing of the breeze it bent
Like a golden ball to bat of chrysolite.

"The Tale of Ali Nur ed-Din
and Miriam the Girdle-Girl,"
Thousand Nights and a Night

THE GRAPEFRUIT AND THE POMELO

Before the nineteenth century there was so such thing as a grapefruit. The earliest mention of it is by a French nobleman, the Chevalier de Tussac, who observed it growing in Jamaica. John Lunan, who also saw it in Jamaica, wrote in 1814 that "it is known by the name of *grapefruit* on account of its resemblance to the grape." A grapefruit neither tastes nor looks like a grape, of course, even a sour one. The reason the grapefruit was so named is obvious when one sees the fruits growing on the tree: they look like giant bunches of bright yellow grapes.

Probably the result of a cross occurring in the wild between a citron and a pomelo, the grapefruit first came into existence in the early 1800s in Jamaica. At first the fruit was thought of as a curiosity and was left to rot where it fell beneath the trees.

Ugli

Pomelo

Gradually the food value of the grapefruit came to be recognized, but the first shipments from Florida to Philadelphia, circa 1885, fetched only 50 cents a barrel!

The largest of citrus fruits, the pomelo originated in the East Indies and Malaya and was brought to the Americas in the seventeenth century. The eminent physician and explorer Sir Hans Sloane, who saw the pomelo growing in the West Indies in 1687–88, described it as being "as big as a man's head." Its shape varies between round and slightly pointed at one end. As with the grapefruit, the skin of the pomelo's segments is thick and easy to remove, but its rind is much thicker than the grapefruit's, being almost as thick as that of the citron. The juice sacs, the largest of any citrus fruit, can be separated when the segments are skinned. A few varieties of the pomelo are pinkish; these are apparently the parents of the pink grapefruit. Pomelos are sweeter than grapefruit, lacking the bitter principle called naringin that gives grapefruit its unique flavor. Usually however, pomelos are not as juicy as grapefruit.

The variety of names given to the pomelo (often spelled *pummelo*) is extremely confusing. Upon discovering it in the East Indies the Dutch named it *pompelmoes* ("big lemon"), from which the modern French name for grapefruit, *pamplemousse*, is derived. Both the grapefruit and the pomelo are referred to in early nineteenth century writings as the shaddock (*shadec* in French), after a Captain Shaddock who, according to Sir Hans Sloane, first brought the seeds to the West Indies. (Historians have sought in vain for proof of Sloane's claim, although a Captain Thomas Chaddock is known to have been governor of the Somers Islands, now the Bermudas, from 1637 to 1641.) The pomelo even has three different Latin names: *Citrus grandis*, *Citrus decumana*, and *Citrus maxima*.

More romantic names for the pomelo are the "Adam's apple" and the "forbidden fruit"; it has been called the latter in both English and French. James Grainger (1721–66) referred to "the golden Shaddock, the forbidden fruit" in a poem about the West Indies. It is not clear why the pomelo was forbidden, but the name is probably due to confusion with the citron, which in Jewish legend was the fruit of the tree of knowledge.

Although good quality is difficult to maintain in pomelos, the Israelis have succeeded in producing a consistently good fruit, which at the time of writing is becoming popular in Europe. Pomelos are being grown commercially in San Diego County in southern California, and may soon be a popular item on American tables. They also still flourish in their original home, the East Indies and Malaya.

The grapefruit is much easier to cultivate than the pomelo. It produces a consistently good crop, and unlike either of its putative parents it is a hardy tree, being particularly resistant to intense heat (strangely, despite being tropical fruits most citrus are susceptible to sunburn). Grapefruit is grown mainly in semiarid areas, consequently, including Israel's northern Negev desert, the Coachella Valley in southern California, and parts of Texas and Arizona.

Though not a desert region, Florida, of course, still produces a sizable crop, and it was here that grapefruit arrived on the American mainland. Count Philippi, a Frenchman who settled in Safety Harbor in Tampa Bay in 1823, distributed seedlings to his neighbors, including a Mr. Duncan, for whom the Duncan grapefruit variety is named. Almost all the yellow and most of the pink grapefruit grown commercially worldwide are descendants of the Philippi seedlings.

The other main grapefruit variety is the Marsh, a seedless descendant of the Duncan. Sports of this variety are the Thompson or Pink Marsh, a pink variety, and the Redblush or Ruby. Pink grapefruit, a recent arrival on the tables of Europe and the United States, have surpassed their yellow cousins in popularity, a fact that has prompted growers to experiment to produce an even deeper pigmentation. The Star Ruby, a variety with ruby red flesh, is the result of irradiation of the Foster Pink seedless variety. The Star Ruby, developed and grown in Texas, is probably the first food to be created through a genetic mutation deliberately produced by radiation.

The strange quirk of public taste that favors the pink-fleshed grapefruit is hard to explain, as the rind of pink-fleshed fruit is often less smooth and less attractive in color than that of the yellow fruit. Rumors have even been spread that the pink

Grapefruit

and ruby varieties are generally sweeter than the yellow, although tests have repeatedly shown this to be untrue. Pink and ruby grapefruit have, however, a much higher vitamin A content than the yellow varieties. Whatever its color, the grapefruit has been outstandingly popular ever since it was first discovered, and will certainly continue to be so.

APPETIZERS

Please note that many dishes in the chapter on salads can also be served as appetizers.

This Greek dish has become a standard item in the cuisine of Mediterranean France. Use the smallest mushrooms available.

Champignons à la Grecque
Marinated Mushrooms
Citrus: lemon

2 tablespoons butter
1 medium onion, chopped fine
2 garlic cloves, minced

½ pound small mushrooms
1 teaspoon oregano
1 teaspoon cayenne pepper
2 lemons, juice squeezed

Melt the butter in a large skillet. Add the onions and garlic and sauté until the onions are transparent. Add the mushrooms and stir to coat them with butter. Add the remaining ingredients, reduce the heat, and cover the pan. Simmer for 5 minutes. Remove from the heat and leave to cool. Serve chilled. Makes 6 to 8 servings.

**Baba Ganouche
(Eggplant Purée)**

Citrus: lemon

This dish is popular in the Mediterranean region wherever eggplants are available. Like all the best Middle Eastern dishes, it is of Turkish origin. The pita bread is used to scoop up the purée, which saves washing utensils.

Tahini, or sesame seed paste, is available at Greek and Middle Eastern grocery stores.

3 eggplants
1 tablespoon salt
½ cup tahini
3 tablespoons caraway seeds

3 garlic cloves, peeled and
   crushed
2 lemons, juice squeezed
½ teaspoon black pepper
3 tablespoons olive oil

Place the eggplants under a broiler or lay them directly on an electric burner. Broil them, turning frequently, until their skins blacken and start to blister. Scrape off the skins with a knife under cold water, removing all the skin and any burned particles. Slice the eggplants several times crosswise, and put the pieces in a bowl of cold water. Sprinkle with the salt and leave for 30 minutes in the refrigerator.

Squeeze the eggplant slices to remove excess liquid. Put them in a blender or food processor and grind them to a smooth paste. Add the tahini, caraway seeds, garlic, lemon juice, and black pepper, and blend again. With the machine running add the oil, and mix until smooth. Spread in a large dish or in individual serving dishes, and garnish with a sprinkle of paprika, lemon wedges, and black olives. Serve with pita bread. Makes 6 to 8 servings.

This elegant dinner party or buffet dish was created by chef Michel LeBorgne of New England Culinary Institute in Montpelier, Vermont, for the 1982 Baltimore Crab Olympics. With this recipe LeBorgne won in the category of Nouvelle Cuisine; he was also overall winner of the whole crab-cooking competition. The original recipe called for *sauce americaine*, a fish sauce containing pounded lobster or crawfish shell—the classic sauce for *lobster à l'americaine*—as one of the mousse ingredients. I have taken the liberty of substituting egg and lemon sauce—it is much simpler to make.

Gâteau de Crabe au Coulis d'Avocat (Seafood Mousse with Avocado Sauce)
Citrus: lime, lemon

SEAFOOD MOUSSE:

1 pound scallops
1 egg white
1½ cups whipping cream
⅓ cup egg and lemon
   sauce (see page 104)

½ teaspoon salt
5 drops Tabasco sauce
½ teaspoon cayenne pepper
1 pound crabmeat

AVOCADO SAUCE:

6 shallots, chopped
1 cup dry vermouth
1 cup chicken broth
3 limes, juice squeezed
3–4 avocados

1 cup whipping cream
3 drops Worcestershire sauce
½ teaspoon salt
5 drops Tabasco sauce

Mince the scallops or put them into a food processor and blend very briefly. Add the egg white, salt, Tabasco, cayenne pepper, and sauce. Gradually add the cream (while the food processor is running, if you are using one). Stir in the crabmeat, then transfer the mixture to a well-greased 1½-quart mold. Place the mold in a pan of warm water so the water comes about a third of the way up the side of the mold. Place the pan in a preheated 325° F. oven and bake for 30 minutes or until set. Remove the mold from the oven, leave it to cool, then refrigerate it until it is firm.

    To make the sauce, put the shallots in a saucepan with the vermouth and broth. Bring them to a boil and cook over medium heat until the liquid is well reduced, about 20 minutes. Remove the pan from the heat and let the contents cool slight-

ly before transfering them to a blender or food processor. Add the lime juice, the flesh of three avocados, and the remaining ingredients, and blend until smooth. The sauce should be fairly liquid, but if it seems to be too runny, add the flesh of another avocado. Taste, and adjust the seasoning.

Unmold the mousse onto a serving platter. Pour some of the sauce around it, so that the mousse appears to be resting on the sauce. Garnish with raw vegetables, such as carrots, green onions, small radishes, and tomatoes, cut into elegant shapes. Serve the rest of the sauce on the side. Makes 8 to 10 servings.

Caribbean Fish Appetizer
Citrus: lime

Pickapeppa sauce is a Jamaican Worcestershire-style sauce. It is available in most supermarkets and in ethnic delis. If you can't find it, use an English "steak sauce" such as O.K. Sauce.

1½ pounds snapper or flounder, cut into ¼-inch cubes
6 limes, juice squeezed and strained
6 drops Pickapeppa sauce
1 tablespoon salt
6 tomatoes
1 cup unsweetened shredded coconut (fresh or packaged)
1 head Boston lettuce

In a glass or ceramic bowl, combine the fish with the lime juice, Pickapeppa sauce, and salt. Pour boiling water over three of the tomatoes to loosen the skins. Skin, seed, and coarsely chop them. Add them to the bowl of fish. Cover the bowl and refrigerate it for at least 12 hours.

2 hours before serving, drain off the marinade (it can be used as a base for cold soup). Skin, seed, and chop the remaining tomatoes, and add them to the bowl with the coconut. Mix well, cover, and refrigerate again. Remove the lettuce heart (save it for salad) and shred the larger leaves. Add them to the mixture 10 minutes before serving. Drain off excess liquid and serve with crackers, tortilla chips, or French bread. Makes 12 servings.

Smoked cod roe is available in the gourmet sections of supermarkets and in Greek and Jewish delicatessens.

Taramasalata (Greek Cod Roe Pâté)
Citrus: lemon

6 slices white bread
6 ounces smoked cod roe
2 tablespoons grated onion

2 garlic cloves, peeled and crushed
½ cup olive oil
2 lemons, juice squeezed

Trim the crusts from the bread and put the slices into a bowl. Add a cup of water and soak the bread thoroughly. Squeeze it to remove excess moisture, discarding the water.

Put the bread, roe, onion, and garlic in a blender or food processor and mix. With the machine running, add the olive oil and lemon juice alternately. When they are completely incorporated, the pâté should be smooth, pale pink, and fluffy.

Transfer the pâté to a serving plate and garnish with parsley sprigs and black olives. Serve with slices of whole-wheat pita bread warmed in the oven. Makes 4 to 6 servings.

A good winter breakfast dish as well as a tasty appetizer.

Hot Spiced Grapefruit
Citrus: grapefruit

4 large grapefruit
4 tablespoons brown suger
½ teaspoon ground allspice
¼ teaspoon ground ginger

1 teaspoon ground cinnamon
2 tablespoons butter, softened
2 tablespoons brandy or triple sec

Cut each grapefruit in half. Use a grapefruit knife to cut the flesh away from the skin and section the grapefruit. Preheat the broiler. In a small bowl, mix the remaining ingredients with a spoon into a smooth paste. Use a metal spatula to spread the paste over the cut surfaces of the grapefruit halves. Arrange the grapefruit on a broiler pan, cut sides. Broil for 5 minutes, or until the cut surfaces of the grapefruit are lightly browned and bubbling. Cool slightly before serving, so the topping forms a crust. For special occasions, decorate with mint leaves. Makes 8 servings.

Smoked Fish Pâté
Citrus: lemon

Smoked fish such as cod, herring (kippers), or whitefish (my favorite) is available in supermarkets, but Jewish delis offer the biggest variety. Smoked tuna can also be used, but it is rather oily, so reduce the amount of olive oil by 2 tablespoons if you use it.

1 pound smoked fish
6 tablespoons heavy cream
6 tablespoons olive oil

1 lemon, juice squeezed
½ teaspoon white pepper

Skin the fish and remove any bones. Put it in a blender or food processor and mix until smooth. With the machine running, add alternate tablespoons of the cream, oil, and lemon juice. Season with pepper. Garnish with parsley and small radishes. Serve with slices of melba toast. Makes 6 to 8 servings.

Hummus (Chickpea Purée)
Citrus: lemon

Another Middle Eastern favorite, this dish is quite filling, so offer small portions if you intend to follow it with a substantial main course.

2 cups chickpeas (garbanzos), soaked overnight in water to cover
3 lemons, juice squeezed
3 garlic cloves, peeled
½ cup tahini

20 black olives, pitted
4 tablespoons chopped parsley
4 hard-cooked eggs, quartered
2 tablespoons olive oil
½ teaspoon paprika

Drain the chickpeas and put them in a saucepan. Cover them with cold water and bring to a boil, uncovered. Cook over medium heat for 1 hour or until tender. Drain the chickpeas, discarding the water and any loose skins.

Put the chickpeas, lemon juice, garlic, and tahini into a blender or food processor. Mix until you have a smooth purée.

To serve, spread the mixture thinly on individual serving dishes. Dribble a little olive oil in the center of each dish and sprinkle with paprika. Garnish with black olives, parsley, and hard-cooked eggs. Serve with pita bread. Makes 4 to 6 servings.

This dish, popular throughout South America, is of Spanish origin. It's therefore best to use olive oil, though any good salad oil will do.

Escabeche de Camarones (Shrimp Marinade)
Citrus: lime

1 cup oil	1 teaspoon dill seed
1 cup wine vineger	½ teaspoon dried tarragon
6 limes, juice squeezed	1 teaspoon dry mustard
2 tablespoons brown suger	½ teaspoon cayenne pepper
5 bay leaves	3 pounds cooked shrimp
6 drops Tabasco sauce	8 red onions, sliced thin

In a large, heavy-based saucepan, put the oil, vinegar, lime juice, sugar, herbs, and spices. Bring to a boil over gentle heat, and simmer uncovered for 10 minutes. Add the shrimp, bring to a boil, and simmer for another 10 minutes.

Drain the shrimp, reserving the liquid. Arrange a layer of onions in a large bowl. Add a layer of shrimp, then another layer of onions, and continue layering until the shrimp and onion are used up. Pour the liquid over the shrimp and onion, making sure it covers them completely. If it doesn't, add more lime juice. Allow to cool and cover the bowl. Refrigerate for at least 2 days before use.

To serve, discard the bay leaves and pile the shrimp and onion on lettuce leaves with 2 tablespoons of the marinade. Serve with tortilla chips or strips. Makes 12 servings.

This classic Mexican dish needs no introduction.

Guacamole (Avocado Dip)
Citrus: lime

2 avocados	1 teaspoon chili powder
2 garlic cloves, peeled	1 lime, juice squeezed
1 teaspoon salt	½ teaspoon Tabasco sauce

Scoop out the flesh from the avocados and put it into a blender or food processor. Add the rest of the ingredients and blend at high speed until smooth. Serve with tortilla chips or strips. Makes 4 servings.

Creamed Cucumber
Citrus: lemon

2 tablespoons salt
3 cucumbers
(about 1 pound)
4 tablespoons chopped chives

1 lemon, juice squeezed and
   strained
2 tablespoons heavy cream
½ teaspoon white pepper

Peel the cucumbers and put them in a bowl of water to cover. Add the salt and soak for 2 hours.

Drain the cucumbers and slice them crosswise into ¼-inch rounds. Sprinkle them with the rest of the salt. Chill the cucumbers for 30 minutes.

Beat the cream with the lemon juice and white pepper until smooth. Rinse the cucumbers to remove excess salt, pat them lightly dry with a kitchen towel, and combine them with the lemon and cream mixture. Serve immediately. Makes 6 to 8 servings.

Chicken Livers with Orange
Citrus: orange

This makes an excellent smorgasbord or buffet dish. The rice is merely a garnish.

6 chicken livers
1 tablespoon butter
1 tablespoon all-purpose flour
3 tablespoons dry white wine
2 tablespoons grated onion
1 teaspoon salt

1 teaspoon black pepper
½ teaspoon dry mustard
1 large orange, sliced
   crosswise in ¼-inch rounds,
   rounds halved
2 tablespoons brown sugar

Melt the butter in a skillet and add the livers. Sauté them over high heat until they are browned, about 5 minutes. Remove them from the pan and arrange them on a serving dish. Keep warm.

Put the flour, wine, onion, salt, pepper, and mustard in the pan and cook 3 minutes, stirring constantly. Remove the skillet from the heat and pour the sauce over the livers. Put the orange slices in the skillet and sprinkle them with the sugar. Cook over moderate heat, turning the slices to coat them evenly with the sugar. When they are glazed, arrange them around the livers. Serve with plain, boiled rice, about 1 tablespoon per person. Makes 6 servings.

A members of the banana family, the plantain strongly resembles the banana we commonly eat as fruit. Plantains have a more "floury" taste than bananas, however, are harder to peel, and can only be eaten cooked. For this recipe they may be used either green or ripe. If you cannot find plantains use green bananas.

2 large plantains	6 tablespoons oil
2½ tablespoons salt	4 limes

Peel the plantains and slice them crosswise at an angle into 1-inch pieces. In a bowl, stir 2 tablespoons of the salt into 5 cups cold water. When the salt has completely dissolved add the plantain slices, and leave for 1 hour.

Drain the plantain slices thoroughly and pat them dry with with towels. Heat the oil in a large skillet. Add the plantains and fry over medium heat until they are tender but not brown, about 10 minutes. Remove them from the skillet, reserving the oil.

Lay the plantain slices on a sheet of wax paper. Lay another sheet of wax paper on top. With a rolling pin, flatten the pieces until they are only ¼-inch thick.

Juice the limes into a bowl and stir in the rest of the salt. Reheat the oil in the skillet. Dip each plantain piece in the lime juice, then sauté it in the oil over high heat until it is crisp and brown, about 3 minutes on each side. Drain the plantain slices on absorbent paper. Transfer them to a serving platter lined with a paper towel to soak up excess oil. Serve immediately. Makes 8 servings.

Plantain Chip Snacks
Citrus: lime

SOUPS

Orange Soup
Citrus: orange

2 tablespoons butter
1 large onion, grated
1 garlic clove, peeled and
    crushed
5 cups beef broth
    (instructions follow)

3 cups tomato juice
5 oranges
1 bayleaf
3 allspice berries
3 drops Tabasco sauce

Melt the butter in a large pan and add the onion. Sauté until the onion is transparent but not browned, and add the garlic. Sauté for 2 minutes, then add the broth, the tomato juice, and the strained juice of three of the oranges. Add the bay leaf, allspice berries, and Tabasco.

Bring the liquid to a boil and simmer for 20 minutes. Slice the remaining oranges, without peeling them, into thin rings. Remove the bayleaf and allspice from the soup and discard it. Pour the soup into individual bowls and decorate with the orange rings. Makes 6 servings.

BEEF BROTH:

2 pounds lean, boneless beef
½ pound veal knuckle or
   chicken bones
2 slices lean ham
bouquet garni (1 bayleaf, 2
   sprigs parsley, and 1 strip
   lemon peel tied in a bunch)

2 onions, 1 stuck with 2 cloves
1 small turnip
2 celery stalks
1 teaspoon salt

Put the meat and bones in a large, heavy pan and add 3 quarts water. Bring to a boil and skim until no scum is left on the surface.

Add the remaining ingredients and simmer very gently for 2½ hours. Strain and refrigerate. Remove the fat from the surface with a spoon or spatula.

Makes 2 quarts.

Watercress Soup
Citrus: lime

1 large or 2 small limes
2 pounds lamb neck slices,
   fat trimmed
3 potatoes, peeled and
   quartered
2 carrots
1 tablespoon long-grain rice
4 tablespoons minced parsley

1 teaspoon thyme
1 bay leaf
½ teaspoon salt
½ teaspoon black pepper
1½ bunches watercress
1 celery stalk, chopped
2 green onions, chopped
4 tablespoons croutons

Cut the lime in half and rub the meat well with the cut surface. Squeeze the rest of the lime juice into a stewpan. Add 2 quarts water and bring to a boil over high heat. Skim any scum that rises to the surface. Reduce the heat, cover the pan, and simmer the meat for 45 minutes. Add the potatoes, carrots, rice, herbs, and seasonings, and cook for 30 minutes. Chop one bunch watercress and add it to the soup with the celery and green onions; cook for 15 minutes. Remove the meat and reserve it for the main course. Pour the soup into individual bowls and decorate it with the rest of the watercress. Makes 8 servings.

Leek and Lemon Soup

Citrus: lemon

2 pounds leeks, trimmed, white parts only
4 tablespoons butter
1 lemon
1 cup celery, chopped coarsely
1 cup spinach, chopped coarsely

4 cups chicken broth (instructions follow)
4 tablespoons minced parsley
4 tablespoons minced coriander leaves
Salt and pepper

Chop the leeks coarsely. In a deep pot melt the butter, and add the leeks and the strained juice of the lemon. Cover tightly and stew over medium-low heat for 10 minutes. Add the chopped celery and cook, covered, for another 10 minutes. Add the spinach and cook, covered, for 2 minutes, or until the spinach has softened. Add the chicken broth, parsley, and coriander, and simmer for 10 minutes. Season to taste before serving. Makes 6 servings.

CHICKEN BROTH:

1 whole chicken or 2 pounds chicken carcasses, giblets, trimmings
1 turnip, quartered
1 onion stuck with 2 cloves

2 celery stalks
1 carrot, split lengthwise
1 bunch parsley
1 teaspoon salt

Put the chicken in a large, heavy pan and cover with water by 3 inches. Bring to a boil and skim any scum from the surface. Cover the pan and simmer for 1½ hours. Add the remaining ingredients and simmer for another 1½ hours.

Strain off the liquid and leave it to cool. When cold, use a spoon or spatula to skim the fat from the surface.

Makes 2 quarts.

Gazpacho is a cold soup from Andalusia, a province of Spain. Since limes are more common than lemons in Mexico, lime juice replaces lemon juice in the Mexican version.

Mexican Gazpacho
Citrus: lime

1 garlic clove, peeled
3 tablespoons olive oil
2 cups beef broth
   (see page 45)
2 cups tomato juice
1 garlic clove, minced
1 cucumber, chopped fine
1 tomato, skinned, seeded,
   and chopped

1 bell pepper, seeded and
   chopped fine
1 lime, juice squeezed
2 soda crackers, crushed
1 tablespoon brown sugar
½ teaspoon salt
5 drops Tabasco sauce

Crush the garlic in a salad bowl. Stir in the olive oil and mix well. Add the broth, tomato juice, garlic, and vegetables, and chill for several hours, covered with plastic wrap. Mix the crushed crackers and sugar with the lime juice and stir until dissolved. Stir into the soup. Season the soup with salt and Tabasco. Put an ice cube in each soup bowl and pour over it. Makes 4 to 6 servings.

Citrus Tomato Soup
Citrus: orange, lemon

2 tablespoons butter
1 onion, chopped coarsely
2 garlic cloves, peeled and
   crushed
1 pound fresh or canned
   tomatoes, peeled, seeded,
   and coarsely chopped

2 cups beef broth
   (see page 45)
2 cups tomato juice
2 oranges
1 lemon
1 bay leaf
4 tablespoons minced parsley

Melt the butter in a large pot and add the onion and garlic. Cook over medium heat until the onion is transparent, about 10 minutes. Add the tomatoes and bring to a boil. Remove the pan from the heat. Allow the contents to cool slightly, then transfer them to a blender or food processor and mix until smooth.

Return the purée to the pot and add the broth and tomato juice. Squeeze the orange and lemon and peel the rinds with a potato peeler. Add the juice, rinds, and bayleaf to the soup. Simmer for 20 minutes. Serve garnished with minced parsley. Makes 6 servings.

Avgolemono Soupa (Greek Egg and Lemon Soup)
Citrus: lemon

This soup could probably be called the Greek national dish. Lemons flourish in the dry climate of Greece and the Greek Islands. As with all national dishes, there are endless variations on the recipe, but the basic method is always the same.

8 cups chicken broth (see page 46)
4 ounces (¼ package) vermicelli

3 large eggs
2 lemons, juice squeezed and strained
Salt and pepper

Heat the broth until it almost boils. Add the vermicelli, and cook for 2 minutes or as long as recommended on the package. Remove the pan from the heat.

Beat the eggs until they foam, and beat the lemon juice into them. Take a ladleful of the hot soup and add it slowly to the egg and lemon, beating constantly. Gradually incorporate two more ladlefuls. Pour the egg and lemon mixture into the soup pot and stir well.

If the soup has cooled too much reheat it, but do not let it boil or it will curdle. Season to taste and serve at once. Makes 8 servings.

Jellied Orange Consommé
Citrus: orange

1 envelope unflavored gelatin
6 cups broth, clarified
1 teaspoon soy sauce

3 oranges
6 sprigs fresh mint

To clarify broth, lightly whip 2 egg whites and crush the shells. Put the broth in a saucepan, and add the whites and shells. Bring the liquid to a boil; when it begins to rise, remove it from the heat briefly. Return it to the heat and simmer for 20 minutes. Strain the broth through cheesecloth.

Stir the gelatin into ⅓ cup of the broth and leave to soften for 10 minutes. Heat the rest of the broth to just below the boiling point. Add the juice of two of the oranges, and remove the pan from the heat. Add the softened gelatin and stir until it is completely dissolved.

Pour the liquid into a bowl and chill until set. Chop the jellied soup lightly and transfer pieces to individual serving bowls. Slice the remaining orange thin, and decorate the bowls with the orange slices and sprigs of fresh mint. Makes 6 servings.

This is an Algerian version of the lemon-flavored chicken soup so popular throughout the Arab countries. *Capelli d'angeli* are very fine vermicelli that can be bought at Italian stores.

1 chicken, cut into serving
  pieces
1 teaspoon black pepper
1 teaspoon salt
1½ tablespoons oil
1 large onion, grated

1 lemon, rind peeled, juice
  squeezed
4 ounces *capelli d' angeli*
2 egg yolks
4 tablespoons minced parsley

Sprinkle the chicken pieces with pepper and salt. Heat the oil in a deep pan and sauté the chicken with the onion. Turn the chicken frequently so it browns evenly. Add a cup of water and cook 10 minutes.

Add a large strip of the lemon peel and 4 cups of water to the pan, and simmer for 30 minutes. Remove the lemon peel, add the *capelli d'angeli,* and cook for 2 minutes or according to package directions.

Remove the pan from the heat. Pour two ladlefuls of the soup into a bowl and beat in the egg yolks. When they are well incorporated, add the lemon juice and parsley. Return the liquid to the soup, stir to incorporate, and remove the pan from the heat immediately, before the soup has a chance to boil. Serve in deep bowls. Makes 4 to 6 servings.

Turkish Wedding Soup

Citrus: lemon

1 pound lean boneless mutton (from the shoulder or boned chops)
2 cups dry red wine
2 teaspoons thyme
2 teaspoons oregano
2 pounds mutton bones with marrow
1 carrot
1 large onion, chopped
6 tablespoons butter
6 tablespoons all-purpose flour
3 egg yolks
1 lemon, juice squeezed
2 teaspoons paprika
1 teaspoon cinnamon

Marinate the meat in the wine and herbs for 8 hours or overnight. Drain the meat, reserving the marinade, and put the meat in a stewpan with the bones, carrot, and onion. Add three quarts water and the reserved marinade. Bring to a boil and simmer for four hours, occasionally skimming any scum that rises to the surface.

Remove the meat and bones. Cut the meat into ½-inch wide strips; discard the bones. Return the meat to the pan.

Melt half the butter in a saucepan. Stir in the flour and cook, stirring constantly, until the mixture is smooth. Add 2 cups soup from the pan and bring to a boil, stirring constantly. Pour this sauce into the soup. Remove the soup from the heat.

Beat the egg yolks with the salt. Gradually add the lemon juice and 1 cup soup. Stir well, then stir this mixture into the soup. Reheat the soup, but do not let it boil or it will curdle.

Just before serving the soup, melt the rest of the butter and stir it with the paprika. Drop a teaspoon of this mixture on each portion of soup, and sprinkle with cinnamon. Makes 12 to 14 servings.

A speciality of the Chinese province of Szechuan. Usually made with vinegar as the sour flavoring, it's at least as good with lemon juice.

Hot and Sour Soup
Citrus: lemon

6 cups vegetable or chicken broth (see pages 56 and 46)
8 ounces tofu, cubed
2 cups shredded cabbage
1 tablespoon soy sauce

2 tablespoons cornstarch
2 lemons, juice squeezed
½ teaspoon cayenne pepper
3 green onions, green parts only, chopped
3 teaspoons sesame oil

Bring the broth to a boil and add the tofu cubes, cabbage, and soy sauce. Reduce the heat and simmer for 5 minutes.

Mix the cornstarch with the lemon juice, cayenne, and 3 tablespoons water. Stir this mixture into the soup and return the soup to a boil. Reduce the heat and simmer for 2 minutes. To serve, pour the soup into individual bowls and sprinkle each with a teaspoon of chopped green onion and a teaspoon of sesame oil. Makes 8 servings.

2 pounds squash or pumpkin, peeled and cubed
3 slices lean bacon
1 celery stalk, chopped
8 peppercorns, tied in cheesecloth
1 bay leaf

2 tablespoons dark brown sugar
3 grapefruits, juice squeezed
1 teaspoon salt
1 teaspoon ground cloves
1 teaspoon black pepper

Squash and Grapefruit Soup
Citrus: grapefruit

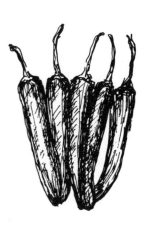

Put the squash or pumpkin, bacon, celery, peppercorns, and bayleaf in a stewpan. Add water to cover (about 2 quarts). Bring to a boil and reduce heat. Cover the pan and cook over medium heat for 40 minutes, or until the squash is soft.

Remove the pan from the heat. Strain the liquid and discard the peppercorns and bayleaf. Put the strained vegetables into a blender or food processor and purée them. Return them to the pan.

Combine the remaining ingredients and add them to the pot. Reheat the soup to just below the boiling point. Serve hot or cold. Makes 6 to 8 servings.

Carrot and Orange Soup

Citrus: orange

This soup will taste just as good, though different, if the cream is omitted.

4 tablespoons butter	8 cups beef broth (see page
1½ pounds carrots, sliced in	45)
thin rings	4 large oranges
4 shallots, chopped	½ cup whipping cream
4 small, white onions, peeled	½ teaspoon salt
but left whole	½ teaspoon black pepper

Melt the butter in a soup pot over medium heat. Add the carrots, shallots, and onions. Reduce the heat and cook, stirring occasionally, for 5 minutes. Cover the pot and cook over low heat for 15 minutes.

Add the broth and simmer for 20 minutes. Remove the pot from the heat, and remove and reserve the onions. Liquefy the soup in a blender. Juice the oranges; grate the rind of one orange and add it to the soup with the juice. Slice the peel of another orange into very narrow strips, removing as much of the pith as possible. Throw these strips into a large pot of salted boiling water and boil for 5 minutes. Drain them.

Pour the soup back into the pot and return it to the heat. Stir in the cream and return the onions to the pot. Reheat the soup, but do not let it boil. Sprinkle the strips of orange peel over the soup just before serving. Makes 4 to 6 servings.

The Chinese serve this soup, as they do their almond soup, at the end of a meal like a dessert. But like Scandinavian fruit soups, it is equally good at the beginning and end of a meal. Glutinous rice flour (also called sweet rice flour) can be obtained at Oriental groceries and in the Oriental foods section of supermarkets.

Chinese Tangerine Soup with Sweet Rice Dumplings

Citrus: tangerine or tangelo, orange flower water

5 large tangerines or tangelos
2 cups glutinous rice flour
½ cup sugar

1 tablespoon orange flower water

Peel the fruit and remove as much connective tissue as possible. Discard the seeds. In a blender or food processor, grind the fruit pulp.

Heat 1½ cups of water until hot but not boiling. Pour it into a bowl and stir in the glutinous rice flour. Beat the mixture until it is smooth. Wet your hands and shape the mixture ino 16 small balls about 1 inch in diameter.

Bring 1 quart of water to a boil. Add the dumplings and boil over brisk heat for 5 minutes. Reduce the heat and add the tangerine pulp and sugar. Cook, stirring, until the sugar has dissolved. Heat to just below the boiling point. Remove from the heat and add the orange flower water. Taste, and add more sugar if desired before serving. Serve hot or cold. Makes 6 to 8 servings.

Green Summer Soup
Citrus: lime

4 cups strong chicken broth, clarified (see pages 46 and 48)
2 large avocados
¼ cup water or clam juice
1 teaspoon soy sauce
2 limes, juice squeezed, rind grated

1 cup sour cream
3 drops green coloring (optional)
2 cups peeled, cooked shrimp
8 tablespoons chopped parsley
½ teaspoon paprika

Pour the broth into an ice tray and chill until partly frozen. Put the avocado flesh, the water or clam juice, the soy sauce, and the lime juice and rind into a food processor or blender and mix until smooth. Gradually add the iced broth and the sour cream. If you prefer a stronger green color, add the food coloring and blend again. Pour the mixture into a bowl, cover with plastic wrap, and refrigerate for at least 2 hours or until ice-cold. To serve, pour the soup into individual bowls and garnish with the shrimp, parsley, and paprika. Lime wedges can be added on the side. Makes 8 servings.

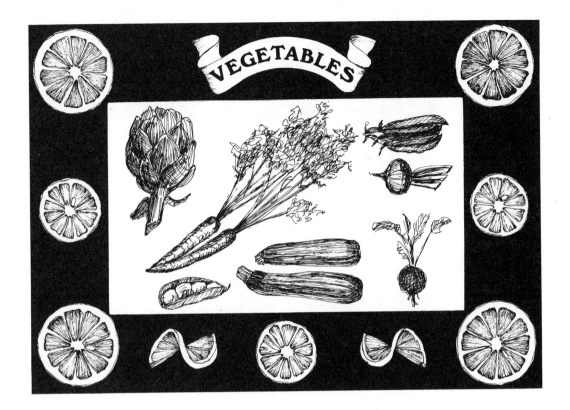

2 pounds medium sweet potatoes	1 tablespoon cornstarch	**Orange-glazed Sweet Potatoes**
½ teaspoon salt	4 tablespoons raisins	*Citrus: orange*
4 oranges	2 tablespoons coarsely chopped walnuts	
4 tablespoons brown sugar	4 tablespoons butter	

Cook the potatoes in boiling salted water until tender, about 20 minutes. Drain and peel them. Slice them in half lengthwise, and arrange them in a greased shallow oven dish. Sprinkle them with the salt.

Mix the brown sugar with the cornstarch and orange juice. Boil, stirring until smooth, then add the raisins. Boil for 5 minutes longer, then remove from the heat and add the chopped nuts. Pour the liquid over the potatoes, and dot them with the butter.

Bake uncovered in a preheated 350°F. oven for 20 minutes, basting at least twice with the sauce during the cooking. Makes 6 servings.

Vegetarian Lemon Rice

Citrus: lemon

4 cups vegetable broth
(instructions follow)
2 tablespoons butter
2 cups Carolina or long-grain
white rice
2 tablespoons oil

½ cup grated sharp Cheddar
cheese
1 egg yolk
1 lemon, juice squeezed, rind
grated

In a saucepan with a tight-fitting lid, heat the broth to the boiling point. Melt half the butter in another pan, and add the rice. Stir until the rice is coated with butter, then add the oil, stirring constantly. Add a ladleful of broth to the rice, and when it boils briskly add another. Keep adding broth this way until it is all used up.

Reduce the heat, cover the rice, and let it simmer, stirring occasionally to prevent sticking. Cook 20 minutes, then add the rest of the butter and the cheese. Mix well and cook for 5 minutes more. Remove the pan from the heat.

Beat the egg yolk with the lemon juice and rind. Stir this mixture into the rice, and return the pan to the heat. Stirring constantly, cook uncovered about 20 minutes, until the rice is tender, but not sticky, and has absorbed all the broth. Makes 4 to 6 servings.

VEGETABLE BROTH:

1 tablespoon butter
3 medium carrots, coarsely
chopped
2 onions, quartered
3 celery stalks, coarsely
chopped

6 peppercorns
1 bay leaf
2 sprigs parsley
1 teaspoon salt

Melt the butter in a large pot and add the carrots, onions, and celery. Cook over medium heat, stirring occasionally, until the butter browns. Add the peppercorns, bay leaf, parsley, salt, and 3 quarts water. Bring to a boil and simmer gently for 3 hours.
Makes 2½ quarts.

3 tablespoons butter
1 celery stalk, chopped fine
3 green onions, chopped fine
3 tablespoons minced parsley
1 large orange, rind grated,
   juice squeezed

1½ cups chicken or vegetable
   broth (see page 46 and
   preceding recipe)
1 teaspoon salt
1 cup long-grain white rice

Orange Rice
Citrus: orange

Melt the butter in a saucepan with a tight-fitting lid. Add the celery, green onion, and parsley and cook, stirring, for 3 minutes. Add the broth, the orange rind and juice, and the salt. Bring to a boil and add the rice quickly. Stir, cover the pan, and reduce the heat. Simmer for 25 minutes or until the rice is tender and most of the liquid absorbed. Makes 4 to 6 servings.

This dish, created by Mrs. Thelma Nuse of Caldwell, Kansas, goes very well with roast pork, ham, or turkey. If you want to brown the turnips while the roast is cooking, bake them at the same temperature as the meat for 20 minutes or so.

Turnips in Orange Sauce
Citrus: orange

2 pounds young turnips
½ teaspoon salt
2 tablespoons brown sugar
2 oranges, juice squeezed

½ teaspoon ground ginger
3 tablespoons butter
1 orange, peeled and divided
   into segments

Put the turnips into a large pan and add water to cover. Add the salt and bring to a boil. Boil until the turnips are tender, about 15 minutes. Drain the turnips (reserve the water for soup base), and purée them in a blender or food processor.

Combine the orange juice, sugar, and ginger. Beat the liquid into the puréed turnips. Transfer the mixture to a small greased oven dish and dot with the butter.

Bake in a preheated 450°F. oven for 10 minutes or until lightly browned on top. Decorate with orange segments before serving. Makes 4 to 6 servings.

Beets in Lime Sauce
Citrus: lime

2 pounds whole raw beets	3 limes, juice squeezed
3 tablespoons brown sugar	1 tablespoon butter
2 tablespoons cornstarch	

Scrub the beets but do not peel them. Put them in a pan of water to cover them. Cook the beets, covered, for 15 to 25 minutes, depending on their size. Test with a knife to see if they are done.

Remove the beets from the pan and continue to boil the liquid, uncovered, until it is reduced by about half. Peel the beets and slice them crosswise neatly. Mix the lime juice with the cornstarch and sugar.

Pour the lime juice mixture into the beet liquid and return it to a boil, stirring constantly until the liquid is smooth. Remove the pan from the heat and stir in the butter. When the butter has melted, add the beets. Serve hot or cold. Makes 6 servings.

Baked Sweet Potatoes with Grapefruit
Citrus: grapefruit

2 pounds small sweet potatoes, unpeeled	2 tablespoons honey
3 yellow grapefruit	½ teaspoon salt
4 tablespoons brown sugar	1 teaspoon cinnamon
	2 tablespoons butter

Boil the potatoes in salted water to cover until they are soft, about 20 minutes. Drain the potatoes, discarding the water.

Peel two of the grapefruit. Discard the skin and as much connective tissue as possible, and chop the pulp coarsely. Squeeze the juice from the third grapefruit.

Combine the juice with the sugar and honey and heat in a saucepan. Add the salt and cinnamon and bring to a boil. Remove the pan from the heat.

Place the potatoes in a greased shallow baking pan, and arrange the grapefruit pulp over and around them. Pour the grapefruit juice mixture over the potatoes. Cut the butter into pieces and sprinkle the pieces on top.

Bake the potatoes in a preheated 350°F. oven for 30 minutes. Makes 4 servings.

1 pound carrots, sliced thin
2 cups chicken broth (see
  page 46)
2 lemons

2 tablespoons sugar
2 tablespoons butter
½ teaspoon ground ginger
1 tablespoon minced parsley

Lemon-glazed Carrots

Citrus: lemon

Pour the chicken broth into a saucepan and add the carrots. Grate the rind from 1 lemon and squeeze the juice. Add the rind and juice to the pan with the sugar, butter, pepper, and parsley. Bring to a boil and cover. Reduce the heat and cook for 30 minutes at a gentle boil, until the liquid has almost evaporated.

Toss the carrots lightly to glaze evenly, and serve hot. Cut the remaining lemon into thin slices, and decorate the dish with them. Makes 4 servings.

In my family, braised red cabbage traditionally accompanies turkey. It is also good with duck, pork, or game.

Braised Red Cabbage

Citrus: lemon, orange

4 tablespoons butter
1 large red cabbage (about 3
  pounds), cored and
  shredded
2 tablespoons orange
  marmalade (see page 115)
2 tart apples, peeled, cored,
  and chopped

1 cup golden raisins
2 lemons, juice squeezed,
  rind grated
4 tablespoons honey
½ cup red wine vinegar
1 teaspoon salt
1 teaspoon black pepper

Melt the butter in a heavy pan or dutch oven. Add the cabbage and marmalade and cook over low heat, stirring constantly, until the cabbage softens. Stir in the apples, raisins, lemon rind and juice, honey, and vinegar. Cover the pan and simmer gently for 1 hour, stirring occasionally.

Before serving, season with salt and pepper and taste for sweetness. Add more honey if necessary to achieve just the right balance between sweet and sour. Makes 6 to 8 servings.

Turkish Artichoke Hearts
Citrus: lemon

This dish may be served hot or cold.

8 globe artichokes	2 garlic cloves, peeled
2 lemons	2 teaspoons sugar
1 teaspoon salt	1 tablespoon cornstarch
2 tablespoons olive oil	

Pour 1 quart water into a large bowl. Cut a lemon in half, and squeeze one half into the water. Add the salt.

Break off the artichoke stems at the base of the vegetable. Remove the outer leaves, pulling away and downward, to leave the fleshy parts behind. When you reach the inner leaves, cut them off with a sharp knife about two-thirds of the way down.

Rub the cut surfaces of the artichokes with the other half of the lemon to prevent discoloring. Pare away the tough outer layer on the bottom of the artichoke, and rub all the cut surfaces with lemon again. Put each artichoke into the bowl of water as you finish with it.

Pour the oil into a large saucepan. Add the garlic, and artichokes. Strain the liquid in which the artichokes were soaked through a cheesecloth and add it to the saucepan. Add the sugar, and bring to a boil. Reduce the heat, cover the pan, and cook for 20 minutes or until the artichokes are tender.

Remove the artichokes from the pan. Continue to boil the cooking liquid, uncovered, for about 20 minutes, so it reduces in volume. Scoop the central leaves and the choke from the artichoke, using your fingers and a teaspoon.

Squeeze the juice from the second lemon and mix it with the cornstarch. When the cooking liquid is well reduced, stir the cornstarch mixture into it. Boil the liquid again, stirring constantly, until it thickens.

Arrange the artichoke hearts in a serving dish. If they are to be served cold, allow the sauce to cool before pouring it over them, then refrigerate the dish until required. If the artichoke hearts are to be served hot, return them to the pan with the sauce to heat them through before serving. Makes 4 servings.

1 cup long-grain white rice
1 teaspoon salt
4 tablespoons oil
½ pound lean ground beef
 or lamb
4 tablespoons minced parsley

1 teaspoon black pepper
24 medium zucchini
2 pounds fresh apricots or
 1 pound dried apricots
4 lemons, juice squeezed

Iraqi Stuffed Zucchini

Citrus: lemon

Soak the rice in water to cover for 1 hour. Drain it well. Parboil the rice for 10 minutes in 3 cups boiling salted water. Drain it.

Heat 1 tablespoon of the oil and brown the meat quickly in it, stirring and turning frequently. Stir in the parsley and pepper and remove the pan from the heat. Stir in the rice.

Cut the zucchini in half lengthwise and scoop out the centers. Pack the zucchini with the rice stuffing and fit the halves back together. Arrange them in a greased shallow oven dish.

If the apricots are fresh, halve them and discard the pits. If they are dried, simply wash them. Arrange the apricots around and between the zucchini.

Pour the lemon juice over the zucchini. Cover the dish with a lid or with foil, and bake in a preheated 325°F. oven for 2 hours. Makes 6 to 8 servings.

2 tablespoons butter
1 onion, chopped fine
1½ pounds Jerusalem
 artichokes, peeled and
 sliced
1 teaspoon salt
½ teaspoon pepper

½ teaspoon grated nutmeg
2 garlic cloves, minced
1 tablespoon minced parsley
1 bay leaf
1 teaspoon dried thyme
4 lemons, juice squeezed

Lemony Jerusalem Artichokes

Citrus: lemon

Heat the butter in a skillet with a lid and fry the onion until it is transparent. Add the artichokes, herbs, and spices. Cover and cook over low heat for 20 minutes, shaking the pan from time to time so the artichokes do not stick to the bottom. Add the lemon juice and ½ cup water and cover the pan again. Cook, stirring occasionally, for 30 minutes. Remove the lid from the pan and boil briskly for 5 minutes to evaporate some of the liquid before serving. Makes 6 to 8 servings.

Malabar Lemon Rice
Citrus: lemon

This is a simplified version of the lemon-flavored rice eaten in southern India, especially in Cochin, the only part of India where lemons, as opposed to limes, are used frequently in cooking. A kind of shortening called *ghee* is usually used in this dish. You can substitute vegetable oil, but if you want to use the real thing, it is available at Indian and Middle Eastern food stores under the name *ghee*, *smen*, or *semneh*, depending on the country of origin. Black mustard seed and curry leaves can be bought at Oriental food stores.

4 tablespoons *ghee* or vegetable oil	2 dried curry leaves
2 small onions, sliced crosswise	1 tablespoon black mustard seed
1 cup long-grain white rice	1 tablespoon blanched almonds
3 cardamom pods	2 tablespoons white raisins
½ teaspoon turmeric	2 lemons, juice squeezed, rind grated
1 stick cinnamon, broken in two	½ teaspoon saffron strands

In a heavy-based saucepan with a tight-fitting lid, heat half the oil. Add the sliced onion, and cook until it is golden brown. Add the rice and stir well. Add the rest of the oil gradually, stirring it into the rice with a wooden spoon until the rice has absorbed it. Add the seeds from the cardamom pods, the turmeric, cinnamon, curry leaves, black mustard seed, almonds, raisins, lemon juice and rind, and 2 cups hot water. Cover the pan and simmer on very low heat until the rice is tender, about 20 minutes.

If all the water has not been absorbed, uncover the pan and cook, stirring for a few moments, so the excess liquid evaporates. Turn the rice into a serving dish and sprinkle with saffron strands. Makes 4 servings.

2 cups long-grain white rice
2 tablespoons salt
6 tablespoons butter, melted
1 pound lean ground beef
  or lamb
1 medium onion, grated
½ teaspoon black pepper
½ teaspoon ground cinnamon

½ teaspon ground nutmeg
1 pound fresh spinach,
  chopped fine
6 tablespoons minced parsley
4 oranges, juice squeezed
1 lemon, juice squeezed
1 tablespoon flour

Persian Rice with Spinach Sauce

Citrus: orange, lemon

Wash the rice thoroughly in warm water to remove excess starch and prevent stickiness. Add 1 tablespoon of the salt to a bowl containing 2 quarts water, and add the rice. Leave it to soak for at least 6 hours or overnight. Drain thoroughly.

Pour 2 quarts of water into a large pan, and bring it to a boil. Add a tablespoon of salt and the rice. Bring the water to a boil again, cover the pan, and boil the rice over low to medium heat for 15 minutes. Transfer the rice to a colander, rinse it in lukewarm water, and drain it thoroughly.

Melt 2 tablespoons of butter in the pan in which the rice was cooked. Add 2 tablespoons water and return the rice to the pan, stirring to coat the grains evenly with butter. Melt another 2 tablespoons of butter, and pour it over the rice. Cover the pan with an absorbent cloth or strong paper towel, then put the lid on the pot. Turn the heat as low as possible and cook 40 minutes.

While the rice is cooking, mix the ground meat with the onion, ½ teaspoon salt, the pepper, and the cinnamon. Shape the mixture into balls about ½ inch in diameter. Melt 2 tablespoons of butter in a skillet and cook the meat balls, turning them frequently until they are lightly browned.

Melt the remaining 2 tablespoons butter in a deep skillet with a lid, and add the spinach and parsley. Sauté the vegetables over medium heat for 5 minutes, then add the meatballs. Add 1 cup water and simmer for 15 minutes, uncovered. Mix the orange juice, lemon juice, and flour, and add this to the meat and vegetable mixture. Cover and simmer for 20 minutes.

Put the base of the pan of rice into cold water to cool the base and stop the cooking process. Turn the rice out into the center of a large deep dish. The brown crust that should have formed on the bottom of the pan will be uppermost, with the white rice below. Pour the spinach and meatball mixture around the rice mound. Makes 4 to 6 servings.

Green Bean and Potato Gratin
Citrus: lemon

3 large potatoes
3 teaspoons salt
1½ pounds green beans
4 tablespoons butter
1 lemon, juice squeezed

1 tablespoon grated onion
½ teaspoon cayenne pepper
1 egg yolk, beaten
2 fresh hot red chili peppers,
   seeded and cut into strips

In a large pan, boil the potatoes with 1 teaspoon of salt in water to cover until they are soft, about 20 minutes.

In another large saucepan, bring 1 cup water to a boil. Add the beans and cook for 15 minutes at a fast boil.

Drain the beans thoroughly (reserve the water for soup). Stir in the lemon juice, the grated onion, half the butter, and toss lightly. Season to taste with salt and cayenne pepper, and toss again. Drain the potatoes (save the water for soup), and mash them thoroughly with 1 tablespoon of the butter and the butter and the egg yolk. Season to taste.

Arrange the beans in a greased oven dish. Spread the potatoes in a smooth layer on top of them, and dot with the rest of the butter. Put the dish under the broiler for 10 minutes or until the potatoes are lightly browned. Garnish with chili pepper strips. Makes 6 to 8 servings.

FISH

This recipe makes a refreshing summer dish. If cod is not available, use other firm, white-fleshed saltwater fish such as halibut, flounder, or whiting.

Cod in Bitter Orange Marinade
Citrus: bitter orange

1 pound cod fillets
1 teaspoon salt
1 onion, sliced thin

4 bitter oranges, juice
  squeezed
½ teaspoon Louisiana-style
  hot pepper sauce

Cut the fish into bite-sized pieces, carefully discarding any remaining bones and skin. Put the pieces into a glass or ceramic bowl (metal may react with the citrus juice), and add the rest of the ingredients. Stir well, and cover with plastic wrap. Leave at room temperature for 2 hours, then refrigerate 2 hours or until needed (but no more than 8 hours). Serve with a green salad. Makes 4 servings.

Court Bouillon for Fish
Citrus: lemon

This is the classic liquid for poaching or steaming fish or shell-fish.

1 lemon, juice squeezed	2 bay leaves
4 sprigs parsley	6 peppercorns
2 sprigs dill (optional)	1 sprig thyme or 1 teaspoon
1 garlic clove (optional)	dried thyme
1 celery stalk	1 teaspoon salt

Put all the ingredients into a large pan. Add enough water to cover the fish to be used. Bring to a boil and simmer for 15 minutes. If you like you can add fish to the court bouillon immediately. Or it can be made in advance and refrigerated till required.

Agristada
(Lemony Fried Fish)
Citrus: lemon

This is a Sephardic Jewish dish for festive occasions.

2 pounds scrod, whiting, or halibut steaks	1 teaspoon salt
	½ teaspoon black pepper
4 tablespoons all-purpose flour	1 teaspoon ground coriander
	1 teaspoon ground cumin
4 tablespoons oil	3 egg yolks
2 lemons, juice squeezed	

Dust the fish slices very lightly with flour. Heat the oil in a skillet with a lid. Add the fish and cook until the flesh is firm, about 5 minutes on each side. Cover the pan and reduce the heat.

Combine the lemon juice with 4 tablespoons water and the salt, pepper, coriander, and cumin. Add this mixture to the pan and cover again. Cook for 15 minutes.

Beat the egg yolks thoroughly. Remove the pan from the heat. Transfer the fish to a serving platter and set in a warm place. Pour the liquid in which the fish slices were cooked over the egg yolks, beating constantly. Return the liquid to the pan and reheat until the liquid thickens, but do not let it boil. Pour a little of the sauce over the fish, and pass the rest separately. Serve immediately. Makes 8 servings.

This recipe is adapted from one in *The Art of Cookery*, written by "a Lady" (who is thought to have been Mrs. Hannah Glasse) and published in 1747. If bitter oranges are not available you can substitute limes. Good accompaniments for this elegant and unusual dish are steamed broccoli and baked Louisiana yams.

Scallops with Bitter Orange Sauce
Citrus: bitter orange

2 pounds scallops	½ teaspoon black pepper
3 bitter oranges	½ teaspoon cayenne pepper
4 tablespoons cream	6 tablespoons butter
3 egg yolks	4 tablespoons flour
½ cup dry white wine	4 tablespoons minced parsley
1 teaspoon salt	

Sprinkle the scallops with the juice of half an orange. Beat the cream, egg yolks, wine, and the juice of 1½ oranges in a bowl, using a wire whisk. Place the bowl in a pan of simmering water and cook, stirring constantly, until the sauce thickens. Remove it from the heat and reserve it in a warm place.

Season the flour with half the salt and the black pepper. Dust the scallops very lightly with flour (the easiest way is by shaking them together in a paper bag). Melt half the butter in a skillet, and sauté the scallops until they are golden brown all over, about 10 minutes. Drain them on absorbent paper.

Reheat the sauce, stirring constantly, but do not let it boil. Cut the rest of the butter into small pieces. Remove the sauce from the heat and stir the butter into it, letting each piece melt before adding another. Season with the rest of the salt and the cayenne pepper.

Arrange the scallops on a serving platter. Cut the remaining orange into wedges, and arrange the wedges between the scallops. Pour a little of the sauce over the center of the dish, and scatter the parsley on top. Serve the rest of the sauce on the side. Makes 6 servings.

Fish Fillets Pamplemousse (Fish Fillets with Grapefruit)

Citrus: grapefruit or pomelo, lime

This is a nouvelle cuisine recipe, as the pink peppercorns indicate. If you can't find them or consider them too expensive, use white peppercorns. Pink peppercorns, which are not peppercorns at all but tiny flower buds, come from the island of Réunion in the Indian Ocean. They are available at gourmet shops.

4 catfish or pompano fillets
½ teaspoon salt
½ teaspoon pepper
1 pink grapefruit or pomelo
1 pint court bouillon
   (see page **66**).
1 lime, juice squeezed, rind grated

1 tablespoon arrowroot or potato starch
1 tablespoon pink peppercorns
3 drops pink coloring (optional)

Season the fish fillets with salt and pepper. Peel the grapefruit or pomelo and skin the segments, reserving the juice. Wrap each fillet around two or three segments, securing it with toothpicks. Save any grapefruit or pomelo segments that are left over for the sauce.

Pour the court-bouillon into a saucepan and add the reserved citrus segments and the lime juice and rind. Put the rolled fish fillets carefully into the pan and cover it. Simmer very gently for 20 minutes.

Remove the fish and reserve it on a serving platter in a warm place. Bring the sauce to a boil, and boil it briskly for 15 minutes or until substantially reduced. Mix the arrowroot or potato starch with ½ cup water and add it to the sauce, stirring constantly, until the sauce thickens. Strain the sauce through cheesecloth and return it to the heat. Add the peppercorns and cook 5 minutes. Add the coloring, if desired, and stir well before removing the pan from the heat.

Discard the toothpicks securing the fish rolls and pour a little of the sauce over them before serving. Serve the rest of the sauce on the side. Makes 4 servings.

For special occasions you can cook a whole rainbow trout as described in this recipe, using a fish kettle. You may need to increase the amount of poaching liquid, in which case you should increase the amount of gelatin proportionately.

Ryba s Sokom (Russian Fish in Aspic)

Citrus: lemon

1 envelope unflavored gelatin
1 tablespoon salt
4 salmon or tuna steaks
3 small carrots
2 celery stalks
1 onion, stuck with 2 cloves

4 sprigs parsley (and root if available)
2 bay leaves
5 black peppercorns
Salt and pepper
3 lemons
1 teaspoon sugar

Soften the gelatin in 1/2 cup warm water. Put the vegetables, herbs, and peppercorns in a large saucepan, and add 2 cups water. Add 1 teaspoon salt and the juice of one of the lemons. Add the fish, cover the pan, and simmer gently for 15 minutes. Carefully remove the fish and leave it to cool. Strain the liquid through cheesecloth.

Add the sugar to the liquid and season with salt and pepper to taste. Return the liquid to the saucepan and heat gently. Add the softened gelatin, and stir until it is dissolved. Remove the pan from the heat, and let the liquid cool to room temperature.

Slice the remaining lemons crosswise as thin as possible. Slice the cooked carrots into rounds. Arrange the fish fillets on a serving platter and decorate with the lemon and carrot slices. Pour half the liquid over the fish and chill in the refrigerator for 45 minutes, or until the liquid has begun to set. Pour the rest of the liquid over the fish and leave it to set in the refrigerator.

Makes 4 servings.

Red Snapper or Yellowtail with Avocado Mayonnaise

Citrus: lemon, lime

2 tablespoons butter
2 pounds red snapper, yellowtail, or scrod steaks or fillets
3 lemons, juice squeezed
2 teaspoons salt
2 avocados
2 tablespoons salad oil
½ onion, grated
½ teaspoon white pepper

Melt the butter in a large pan with a tight-fitting lid. Add the fish, the juice of 2 of the lemons, and half the salt. Cover the pan and reduce the heat. Simmer the fish over low heat for 20 minutes, shaking the pan occasionally.

To make the mayonnaise, scoop the flesh from the avocados and purée it in a food processor or blender. With the machine running add the rest of the salt, the juice of the third lemon, and the remaining ingredients. Blend until smooth.

Arrange the fish on a serving platter and pour a little of the mayonnaise over it. Serve the rest on the side. Decorate the fish with watercress or parsley. Serve hot or cold. Makes 8 servings.

Porgy with Pickled Lemon

Citrus: lemon

4 lemons
4 tablespoons coarse salt
1 cup olive oil
1 large whole porgy or 2 small ones (about 3 pounds total)
1 teaspoon ground coriander
1 tablespoon paprika

The day before the fish is to be cooked, slice the lemons crosswise into rounds, discarding the ends. Arrange the rounds on a dish, and sprinkle them with half the salt and 2 tablespoons of the oil. Leave at room temperature, lightly covered, for 8 hours. Then turn the lemons over and sprinkle them with the rest of the salt and 2 more tablespoons of the oil. Leave for at least 8 hours or overnight.

Wash the fish and make a small incision at the base of the head. Gut the fish through the incision so as to leave it whole. Arrange half the lemon slices on an oiled oven dish, and lay the fish on top of them. Arrange the remaining lemon slices over the fish. Mix the coriander and paprika with the oil and sprinkle it over the fish. Preheat the broiler.

Broil the fish, basting frequently, until the flesh is firm and lightly browned. Makes 8 servings.

This recipe makes a good appetizer as well as a main dish.

Fried Marinated Fish
Citrus: lime

1½ pounds Pacific red snapper, catfish, or pompano fillets
5 limes
4 tablespoons all-purpose flour
1 teaspoon salt
½ teaspoon chili powder
5 tablespoons oil

1 red onion, sliced thin
1 tablespoon sugar
2 bell peppers, seeded and sliced thin
1 mild green chili, seeded and sliced thin
1 medium pickled cucumber, chopped fine
3 tablespoons capers

Cut the fish into serving pieces. Slice 1 lime in half and rub the fish thoroughly with the cut surfaces. Leave for 10 minutes at room temperature.

Toss the flour in a paper bag with the chili powder and 1 teaspoon of the salt. Put the pieces of fish in the bag, one by one, and toss them in the seasoned flour.

Heat 4 tablespoons oil in a large skillet and fry the fish until it is golden brown all over, about 10 minutes on each side. Drain the fish on absorbent paper.

In a saucepan combine the juice of the remaining limes with the onion, sugar, bell peppers, mild chili, and the rest of the oil. Bring to a boil, reduce the heat, and cook 5 minutes. Add the capers and pickles. Remove from the heat.

Put the fish in a large bowl and pour the marinade over it. When cool, cover with plastic wrap and refrigerate for at least 24 hours, or until needed. Makes 6 servings.

Halbut, Jewish Style
Citrus: lemon

Fish liver can be bought from good fishmongers; order one in advance.

2 tablespoons oil
2 onions, sliced thin
6 halibut steaks
1½ teaspoons salt
3 lemons, juice squeezed
8 ounces fish liver
3 eggs

2 tablespoons bread crumbs
   or fine matzo meal
1 tablespoon chopped parsley
½ teaspoon black pepper
1 tablespoon cornstarch or
   potato starch

Heat the oil in a stewpan. Add the onions and sauté until they are transparent, about 10 minutes. Add the fish and sprinkle it with 1 teaspoon salt and the juice of 1 lemon. Cook for 5 minutes, then add enough water to cover the fish (about 3 cups). Cover the pan and cook over a low heat for 10 minutes.

While the fish is cooking, boil the fish liver briskly in salted water to cover. Drain the liver, and chop it fine or grind it. Add 1 egg, the breadcrumbs or matzo meal, the parsley, the remaining salt, and the pepper, and mix until smooth. With floured hands, mold the mixture into small dumplings, each about the size of a walnut.

Add the dumplings to the pan with the fish and cook, simmering for 12 to 15 minutes.

Carefully remove the fish and arrange it in the center of a serving dish. Garnish with the dumplings.

Strain the liquid in which the fish was cooked. Mix the cornstarch with the juice of the remaining lemons. Add 2 cups of the liquid; if there is not enough to make 2 cups, add water to make up the difference. Pour the liquid into a saucepan and bring to a boil over medium heat, stirring constantly. Cook 3 minutes, then remove the pan from the heat and let it cool while you beat the two remaining eggs. Pour the liquid over the eggs, return the pan to the lowest possible heat, and stir until the liquid thickens. Do not let it boil or it will curdle.

Let the sauce cool slightly, then coat the fish with it. Serve lukewarm or cold. Makes 6 servings.

This classic French recipe, which is simplicity itself, can be applied to any saltwater fish fillet.

Sole à la Meunière (Sole Fried in Butter)
Citrus: lemon

4 tablespoons butter
2 sole fillets

½ lemon, juice squeezed

Melt half the butter in a skillet, and heat it until it is very hot. Add the fish and panfry about 2 minutes on each side. The flesh should be firm but not colored.

Transfer the fish to a serving platter and keep it warm. Melt the rest of the butter and pour it over the fish. Sprinkle with the lemon juice. Serve immediately. Makes 2 servings.

Crab Pie
Citrus: lemon

If you get your crabmeat from a freshly-cooked Dungeness crab or similar large-shelled crab, the mixture can be packed back into the crab shell, broiled, and served. Other crabmeat (such as meat from the blue crab) should be baked in a pie shell or pastry case, as the shell will not be large enough to hold the meat.

About ½ pound cooked
   crabmeat (or meat from
   1 large crab)
1 teaspoon salt
½ teaspoon black pepper
¼ teaspoon grated nutmeg
1 tablespoon bread crumbs

1 lemon, juice squeezed
1 teaspoon Dijon-style
   mustard
1 tablespoon unsalted butter
1 8-inch pie crust, prebaked
   (optional)
4 teaspoons minced parsley

Flake the crabmeat with a fork and combine it with the salt, pepper, nutmeg, breadcrumbs, lemon juice, and mustard. Cut the butter into small pieces and beat it into the mixture. Pile the mixture into the pie shell or crab shell and broil it under medium heat for 5 minutes or until brown. Garnish with minced parsley. Makes 8 to 10 servings.

**Broiled Sole
in Orange Sauce**
Citrus: orange

This dish is very good with creamed potatoes and a cooked green vegetable.

3 tablespoons butter
1 onion, chopped fine
2 large oranges
4 large sole fillets
1 tablespoon oil

1 tablespoon minced
   coriander (cilantro)
½ teaspoon salt
½ teaspoon white pepper
1 teaspoon herb vinegar
6 sprigs parsley

To make the sauce, melt 1 tablespoon of the butter in a saucepan. Add the onion and cook over medium heat for 10 minutes, or until the onion is transparent. Meanwhile, grate the rind of half an orange. When the onion is ready, add the orange rind to the pan with the juice of a whole orange. Bring to boil and remove the pan from the heat.

Brush a broiler rack or barbecue grill with the oil. Lay the fish on the broiler or barbecue, skin side away from the heat. Melt the rest of the butter and brush it over the fish. Sprinkle it with coriander, salt, and pepper.

Broil the fish until the surface is lightly browned. Transfer it to a warmed serving platter. Cut the reserved orange into quarters and use it to garnish the fish. Keep warm.

Return the sauce to the heat and add the herb vinegar. When the sauce is hot but not boiling, pour it over the fish. Garnish with the parsley sprigs. Serve immediately. Makes 4 servings.

MEAT

		Israeli Chicken
1 large roasting chicken	1 lemon, juice squeezed	*Citrus: orange*
2 oranges (Jaffas, if possible)	4 tablespoons soy sauce	
4 tablespoons honey	½ onion, grated	
½ teaspoon ground ginger	½ cup slivered almonds	

Put the chicken in a roasting pan with 1 cup water. Peel one of the oranges and stuff the whole orange inside the chicken. Squeeze the juice of the remaining orange and combine it with the honey, ginger, lemon juice, soy sauce, and onion. Pour this mixture over the chicken.

Roast the chicken in a preheated 400° F. oven for 30 minutes, basting at least once with the cooking juices. Reduce the heat to 350° F. and cook for 45 minutes, basting every 15 minutes. Sprinkle the chicken with the almonds and bake for 30 minutes, or until the almonds are browned and the chicken is cooked through.

Serve with rice. Makes 6 servings.

Tropical Stuffed Roast Pork

Citrus: orange, lime

Ripe plantains are completely black skinned and look rather unappetizing if you are not used to them. If you cannot get plantains, use ripe (not overripe) bananas.

4 tablespoons butter
2 ripe plantains, sliced
 in ½-inch rounds
4 slices white bread, crusts
 removed
1 orange, rind grated, juice
 squeezed
1 teaspoon chili powder

1 lime, rind grated, juice
 squeezed
1 cup walnuts
1 ripe mango, peeled, flesh
 coarsely chopped
2 teaspoons salt
1 boneless pork loin
 (about 5 pounds)

Melt the butter and fry the plantains in it until they are golden. Reserve the melted butter, and chop the fried plantains coarsely. Combine the orange and lime juice and soak the bread in this mixture. Grind the walnuts. Mix the butter, plantains, soaked bread, any remaining juice, walnuts, mango, and seasonings. If the mixture is too dry to cohere in a ball, add more citrus juice; if it seems runny, add fresh bread crumbs or ground nuts.

Preheat the oven to 400°F. Spread out the loin on a board and cover the surface with the stuffing mixture. Roll it up and tie it securely with string to ensure the stuffing does not escape. Stick skewers in each end for good measure.

Put the loin in a roasting pan with ½ cup water. Cook the meat, turning every 10 minutes, until it is browned all over, about 30 minutes. Reduce the oven temperature to 325°F. and continue cooking for about 2 hours, or until the meat is thoroughly cooked.

Serve with yams and plantains that are sliced lengthwise, dotted with butter, and baked.

You can order both suet (beef kidney fat) and sausage casings from a good butcher or find them at a big butcher's store in a farmers' market. Instead of using sausage casings, if you wish you can make sausage patties, wrap them in caul fat (also obtainable from a good butcher), and fry them.

Herb and Lemon Sausages
Citrus: lemon

3 pounds lean boneless pork
3 pounds leans boneless veal
2 pounds beef suet
1 teaspoon black pepper
1 teaspoon cayenne pepper
1 tablespoon salt
1 teaspoon marjoram
1 tablespoon grated nutmeg

1 teaspoon ground sage
1 teaspoon ground thyme
2 teaspoons dried ground
   lemon rind (optional)
1 lemon, rind grated, juice
   squeezed
½ pound sausage casings

Chop the pork, veal, and suet roughly. Grind them in a meat grinder or food processor. Add the remaining ingredients and grind again until the mixture resembles a thick, smooth paste.

Run cold water through the casings to clean and open them. To stuff each casing, roll it over the neck of a funnel. Press the sausage meat through the funnel and into the casing, making sure the casing is filled evenly to within 2 inches of the end farthest from you. When the casing is filled, knot the far end securely. Roll the sausage on a table to distribute the contents evenly, then make it into links by twisting every 6 inches, in alternate directions to prevent it unwinding.

Prick the sausages to prevent bursting. Poach them in barely simmering water for 20 minutes if they are not going to be fried immediately. Makes about 45 sausages.

**Iraqi Chicken
and Rice**

*Citrus: lime, orange
flower water*

This recipe uses the dried limes referred to in the first chapter. They can be found at many Middle Eastern food stores, particularly those catering to Iraqis and Armenians. You can easily dry your own limes by leaving them in a warm place, such as over a gas stove or on top a radiator, for two weeks or so, until they are hard and brittle. Then crush them with a rolling pin or in a mortar.

Garam masala is an Indian spice mixture available in the international sections of supermarkets and at Middle Eastern food stores.

4 limes, dried or fresh
1 frying chicken, 3 to 3½
   pounds, cut into serving
   pieces
3 onions, 1 cut in half, 2 in
   thin rounds
1 carrot, split lengthwise
1 leek, split lengthwise
4 eggs
1 cup golden raisins
4 tablespoons butter
½ cup slivered almonds

¼ cup pine nuts (pignolias)
1 tablespoon salt
1 teaspoon chili powder
   (Indian if possible)
2 tablespoons garam masala
1 teaspoon ground coriander
1 teaspoon ground allspice
4 cups long-grain white rice
1 tablespoon orange flower
   water
1 teaspoon powdered saffron
salt and black pepper

If you are using dried limes, break them into pieces and boil them in 1½ cups water for 10 minutes. Soak the pieces of chicken in the water with the limes for 30 minutes before cooking. If you are using fresh limes, squeeze the juice and mix it with ½ cup water, then marinate the chicken in this liquid for 30 minutes.

Put the chicken, marinade, vegetables, and eggs in their shells in a large pot, and add water to cover. Cover the pot, bring to a boil, and simmer the contents 30 minutes.

While the chicken continues to cook, remove the eggs from the pan and cool them under running water. Peel the eggs, being careful to leave them whole, then set them aside to cool.

Soak the raisins in ½ cup of the hot broth for 10 minutes.

Drain throughly, returning the broth to the pot with the chicken.

Melt the butter and sauté the nuts and raisins until the nuts are lightly browned. Remove them from the pan, reserving the melted butter in the pan. Add the onions to the pan and sauté them until they are transparent, then combine the salt, chili powder, garam masala, coriander, and allspice, and stir the mixture into the onions. Quarter the hard-cooked eggs and add them to the mixture. Fry for 5 minutes, then remove from the heat and reserve.

Bring 6 cups salted water to a boil and add the rice. Cover, and parboil over low heat for 10 minutes. Drain the rice and rinse it under cold running water.

When the chicken has been cooking 1½ hours or is tender, remove it from the pot and strain the broth. Pour 4 cups broth (or broth and water, if the broth alone does not make up 4 cups) into a pan, and add the orange flower water, the saffron, and salt and pepper to taste. Bring to a boil, add the rice, and cook 10 minutes, or until the rice has absorbed most of the liquid.

Pile the rice on a serving platter, arrange the chicken pieces around it, and garnish with the hard-cooked eggs and onions. Sprinkle the nuts and raisins on top. Makes 6 servings.

Brazilian-style Rabbit

Citrus: bitter orange

1 rabbit, jointed
2 tablespoons all-purpose
  flour
2 tablespoons oil
1 cup chicken broth
  (see page 46)
1 bitter orange, rind grated,
  juice squeezed
2 small hot green chilies,
  seeded and chopped
2 tomatoes, skinned, seeded,
  and chopped
2 tablespoons minced parsley
½ teaspoon ground ginger

Dust the rabbit pieces with the flour. Heat the oil in a deep pan and fry the rabbit until it is browned all over, turning frequently. Add the remaining ingredients and bring the liquid to a boil. Cover the pan, reduce the heat, and simmer until the rabbit is tender, about 1 hour.

Makes 4 servings.

Lemon and Lime–glazed Cornish Hens

Citrus: lemon, lime

3 cornish hens, split in half
Salt and black pepper
1 lemon, rind grated, juice
　squeezed
½ cup honey

1 lime, rind grated, juice
　squeezed
¼ teaspoon ground ginger
¼ teaspoon pumpkin pie
　spice

Preheat the oven to 400° F. Sprinkle the cornish hens all over with the salt and pepper. Lay them cut side down in a shallow roasting tray. Roast them for 30 minutes.

Meanwhile, combine the grated rinds, juices, honey, and spices. Reduce the oven temperature to 325° F., and baste the birds thoroughly with the mixture. Roast the hens for another hour, basting every 15 minutes with the pan juices.

Remove the hens to a serving platter. Garnish with extra slices of citrus fruit and fresh greens before serving. Makes 6 servings.

Moroccan Meatballs

Citrus: lemon

4 slices white bread, crusts
　removed
1½ pounds lean ground
　beef
1 onion, chopped fine
½ teaspoon salt
½ teaspoon black pepper
4 tablespoons minced parsley

½ teaspoon nutmeg
1 egg
3 tablespoons all-purpose
　flour
2 tablespoons olive oil
2 egg yolks
2 tablespoons heavy cream
1 lemon, juice squeezed

Soak the bread in half a cup of water and squeeze out the excess moisture. Combine the bread with the meat and onion and season with the salt, the pepper, the parsley, and the nutmeg. Add 1 egg and beat until well combined. Shape the mixture into balls about 1 inch in diameter. Toss the balls in the flour.

In a saucepan, heat the oil with 2 cups water. When the liquid boils, add the meatballs and cook them for 30 minutes.

In a bowl, beat the egg yolks with the heavy cream and the rest of the salt, and gradually beat in the lemon juice. Remove the pan containing the meatballs from the heat and pour the egg and lemon mixture over the meatballs, stirring vigorously. Serve with steamed rice. Makes 6 servings.

If bitter oranges are not available, use 3 lemons and 3 limes.

Mexican-style Pork Chops

Citrus: bitter orange

6 bitter oranges
8 center-cut pork chops
1 teaspoon salt
1 teaspoon black pepper
1 teaspoon chili powder

..easpoon Dijon-style
  mustard
¼ teaspoon Louisiana-style
  hot pepper sauce
¼ teaspoon ground
  cinnamon

Grate the rind and squeeze the juice of 4 of the oranges, discarding the seeds. Cut the remaining 2 oranges crosswise into 6 slices each, discarding the first and last, which contain little or no pulp.

Sprinkle the chops with the salt, pepper, and chili powder. Brown them on both sides in a skillet with a lid. Mix the remaining ingredients and pour them over the chops. Cover the skillet, reduce the heat, and simmer the chops for 20 minutes. Remove the chops from the pan, arrange them on a serving dish, and keep them warm. Increase the heat and cook the sauce, stirring occasionally, until it is reduced to a syrupy consistency, about 15 minutes.

Place an orange slice on each chop and pour the sauce over. Makes 4 servings.

Mandarin Chicken
Citrus: mandarin

This dish is easiest made in an electric skillet. Orange bitters are available at good liquor stores.

2 tablespoons butter
1 chicken, cut into serving
  pieces
1 celery stalk, chopped fine
1 small onion, chopped fine
1 cup chicken broth
2 tablespoons orange bitters

5 mandarins
1 teaspoon dried marjoram
1 teaspoon dried oregano
1 tablespoon cornstarch
2 tablespoons brown sugar
2 tablespoon soy sauce

Melt the butter and fry the chicken pieces in a deep skillet with a lid until well browned. Remove the chicken and reserve it. Add the celery and onion to the pan and cook until the onion is transparent, stirring frequently. Add the chicken broth, bitters, and the grated rind of 1 mandarin. Bring to a boil, then reduce the heat to simmer the contents. Add the herbs. Combine the cornstarch, brown sugar, and soy sauce with the juice of 1 mandarin and add to the liquid, stirring constantly until the liquid boils again.

Return the chicken to the pan and cover it. Cook over low heat for 45 minutes.

Peel and section the remaining mandarins, discarding as much skin and connective tissue as possible. Decorate the chicken with the mandarin segments. Makes 6 servings.

A *tagine* is a kind of North African stew. It gets its name from a pot with a conical lid, in which it is cooked.

Moroccan Chicken Tagine
Citrus: lemon

3 pickled lemons
  (see page 107)
2 cups green olives, pitted
4 tablespoons olive oil
1 chicken, cut into serving
  pieces
2 onions, chopped
2 tomatoes, peeled, seeded,
and chopped
2 garlic cloves, peeled and
  minced
½ teaspoon powdered
  saffron
4 tablespoons minced fresh
  coriander (cilantro)
1 teaspoon cayenne pepper

Rinse the olives and lemons thoroughly in warm water to remove excess salt.

Heat the oil in a large, deep skillet with a lid. Fry the chicken pieces, turning them frequently, until they are golden brown. Remove the chicken pieces and replace them with the onion. Cook the onion until it is transparent, then add the tomatoes, garlic, saffron, and coriander. Return the chicken to the pan, and season it with the cayenne. Add 1 cup water, the olives, and the lemon slices.

Cover the pan and simmer the contents for 1 hour, or until the chicken is tender. Or transfer the mixture to a casserole and bake it in a preheated 325° F. oven.

Makes 6 servings.

**Duckling
Maltese Style**
Citrus: blood orange

If blood oranges are not available, ordinary sweet oranges can be substituted, with a little red coloring added to the sauce.

1 duckling	1 teaspoon cornstarch
1 tablespoon salt	1 teaspoon black pepper
3 blood oranges	1 bunch watercress
1 cup dry red wine	

Preheat the oven to 400°F. Sprinkle the duckling with the salt, inside and out, and roast it in a baking dish for 30 minutes. Remove the duck from the oven and drain off the fat. Reduce the heat to 350°F., and return the duck to the pan. Add 1 cup water and continue to cook for 1½ hours or until the bird is tender and well browned.

While the duck is cooking, thinly peel the rind from the oranges and slice it into very thin strips. Put the rinds into a pan of cold water and bring to a boil. Drain the rinds and rinse them under cold water. Repeat this process twice, then set the rinds aside. Squeeze the juice from the oranges and mix it with the cornstarch.

Remove the duck from the pan and put it on a serving platter. Skim the surface of the pan with a paper towel to remove as much fat as possible. Then place the pan on top of the stove over low heat. Stir and scrape the pan to dislodge any bits sticking to the bottom, and add the wine. Bring to a boil and add the orange juice and cornstarch mixture. Cook, stirring, until the sauce is thick. Add the reserved rinds and the pepper. Pour the sauce into a sauceboat and keep it warm.

Carve the duck into serving pieces, and garnish with the watercress. Pour a little sauce over the pieces and hand the rest separately. Makes 6 servings.

1 pound lean ground beef
1 medium onion, grated
2 teaspoons salt
1 teaspoon ground
  coriander
1 teaspoon ground cumin
½ teaspoon black pepper
½ teaspoon cinnamon
6 tablespoons butter

2 garlic cloves, minced
1 pound fresh spinach
  chopped fine
6 tablespoons parsley,
  minced
4 oranges, juice squeezed
2 lemons, juice squeezed
1 tablespoon flour

Persian Meatballs

Citrus: orange, lime

In a large bowl combine the meat, onion, 1 teaspoon salt, coriander, cumin, black pepper, and cinnamon. Mix well. Shape the mixture into balls about 1 inch in diameter.

Melt 4 tablespoons of the butter in a saucepan with a lid. Fry the meatballs, turning frequently until the meat is evenly browned, about 10 minutes. Remove the meatballs and drain them on absorbent paper. Put the rest of the butter in the pan and add the garlic, spinach, and parsley. Cook on high heat for 5 minutes, or until the spinach is wilted. Return the meatballs to the pan and add 1 cup water. Cover and simmer over low heat for 15 minutes.

Combine the orange and lemon juice with the flour and the rest of the salt. Add the mixture to the pan and stir. Serve with steamed rice. Makes 4 servings.

Crown Roast of Lamb with Kumquats
Citrus: kumquat, lemon

2 racks of lamb consisting of 6 cutlets each, trimmed
1 pound kumquats
1 cup fresh bread crumbs
4 tablespoons fried bacon, crumbled
1 large onion, grated
1 teaspoon ground sage
1 teaspoon ground marjoram
1 egg, beaten
½ teaspoon black pepper
½ teaspoon salt
4 tablespoons honey
2 tablespoons lemon juice

Curve the two racks of lamb into a ring, and tie securely with string.

Reserve 12 kumquats, and remove seeds from the rest. Chop the seeded kumquats coarsely and mix them with the breadcrumbs, bacon, onion, and herbs. Bind the mixture with the egg, so it becomes a smooth purée. If it seems too dry, add a tablespoon or two of water.

Arrange the lamb on a roasting dish and put the stuffing in the center. Mix the honey and lemon juice, and brush the outside of the meat with this mixture. Put the meat in the preheated 350° F. oven, and after 15 minutes reduce the heat to 375° F. Roast for 45 minutes more or until the meat is browned, basting twice with the pan juices.

Remove the meat from the oven. Slice off the stem end of the reserved kumquats and stick each one over an exposed cutlet bone. Baste the kumquats with the pan juices and return the lamb to the oven for 5 minutes.

Serve in the roasting dish if possible. Makes 6 servings.

1 small ready-to-eat boneless
   ham (about 8 pounds)
3 grapefruit

1 cup dry white wine
½ cup honey
1 tablespoon cornstarch

Grapefruit-glazed Ham

Citrus: grapefruit

Preheat the oven to 325° F. Put the ham in a roasting pan, fat side up. Bake it for 1½ hours. Remove the ham from the oven and increase the temperature to 375° F. Carefully remove the skin from the ham and score the fat into diamonds.

Squeeze the juice from 2 of the grapefruit and combine it with the wine and honey. Pour this liquid over the ham, and return the ham to the oven. Bake it for 40 minutes, basting every 10 minutes with the liquid. While the ham is cooking, peel and section the remaining grapefruit, discarding as much of the skin and connective tissue as possible.

Remove the ham from the oven and transfer it to a serving platter. Put the pan on the stove over low heat. Combine the cornstarch with ½ cup water and add to the pan juices. Cook, stirring constantly, until the liquid boils and thickens. Pour it over the ham.

Garnish with the reserved grapefruit sections. Makes 10 to 12 servings.

Simple Grapefruit Salad
Citrus: grapefruit

2 large yellow or pink
   grapefruit
¼ cup olive oil
2 tablespoons white or red
   wine vinegar (depending
   on grapefruit color)
1 teaspoon fennel seed

½ teaspoon salt
½ pound radish, daikon,
   or jicama
2 green onions, chopped
1 large garlic clove, peeled
1 tablespoon sunflower seeds,
   raw or roasted

Peel the grapefruit and discard all the skin and connective tissue. Break the flesh into chunks.

Combine the oil, vinegar, fennel, and salt. Cover tightly and chill. Grate or shred the radish, daikon, or jicama, and combine with the grapefruit and green onions. Chill separately.

Just before serving, rub the salad bowl with the garlic clove. Add the grapefruit mixture, then add the dressing and toss. Sprinkle with the sunflower seeds. Serve immediately. Makes 4 servings.

Other shellfish or mock lobster (monkfish), precooked in court bouillon (see page 66), can be used in this recipe instead of lobster. You will need about 1 pound fish flesh. Daikon can be bought at Oriental food stores.

Avocado Lobster Salad

Citrus: grapefruit

1 cooked lobster	½ teaspoon salt
3 avocados	½ teaspoon black pepper
½ cup mayonnaise	1 lemon, juice squeezed
(see page 99)	1 pound jicama or daikon
2 hard-cooked eggs	Salt-free citrus spice
2 limes, juice squeezed	(see page 113)

Remove the flesh from the lobster and cut it into bite-sized chunks. In a blender or food processor combine the avocado flesh with the mayonnaise, hard-cooked eggs, lime juice, salt, and pepper, until you have a smooth sauce. Slice the jicama or daikon into neat rounds; if you are using jicama, slice the vegetables crosswise, then cut out rounds with a cookie cutter. Sprinkle with the lemon juice.

Arrange the jicama or daikon rounds around the inside edge of individual salad dishes. Pile the lobster meat in the center. Sprinkle the lobster with salt-free citrus spice. Pour a little of the sauce over the lobster, so that some of the meat still shows. Serve the rest of the sauce on the side. Makes 4 to 6 servings.

Oriental Tangerine Salad

Citrus: tangerine or tangelo

4 tangerines or tangelos	2 tablespoons soy sauce
4 carrots	2 tablespoons sesame oil
2 tablespoons rice vinegar	2 tablespoons sesame seeds
or herb vinegar	

Peel the tangerines or tangelos. Break them into segments, removing seeds, pith, and as much of the skin around the segments as possible. Grate or shred the carrots and combine them with the fruit.

Mix the vinegar, soy sauce, and sesame oil, beating thoroughly. Pour this over the tangerine and carrot mixture and sprinkle with sesame seeds. Makes 4 servings.

Munkaczina
Citrus: blood orange

The origin of this salad remains obscure. It has been referred to as French and even Arabian, but the name indicates that it comes from further west, from Munkacz. Munkacz is a town in the part of eastern Europe that is constantly changing hands. At present it is in the USSR; it has also belonged, at various times, to Hungary and Romania. Munkacz lies in the region known as Transylvania, which, while not notorious for its oranges, is certainly notorious in other ways. In honor of its most famous son (Dracula, of course!), this version of Munkaczina is made with blood oranges.

2 blood oranges
1 medium red onion,
 chopped fine
1 teaspoon olive oil

4 tablespoons black olives,
 pitted
½ teaspoon cayenne pepper
½ teaspoon salt

Slice the oranges crosswise without removing the peel. Peel the slices and remove and discard the central core.

Arrange the orange slices in a shallow dish and sprinkle the onion over them. Slice the olives in half and sprinkle them over the onion. Sprinkle the salad with the cayenne, salt, and olive oil. Makes 4 servings.

**Orange and
Avocado Salad**
Citrus: orange, lime

4 oranges
2 avocados
2 limes, juice squeezed
4 tablespoons olive oil

1 teaspoon salt
½ teaspoon black pepper
12 black olives, pitted

Slice the oranges crosswise and remove the peels. Arrange orange slices around the edges of four individual salad plates. Remove the flesh from the avocados and dice it. Squeeze the lime juice over it, and add the salt and pepper. Divide the avocado flesh between the four plates, piling it in the center of each. Top each plate with 4 black olives, and serve immediately. Makes 4 servings.

This is a good salad for a picnic or buffet, when you have to cater for a large party. It is an unusual alternative to cole slaw.

Pineapple and Grapefruit Salad

Citrus: yellow grapefruit, orange

1 pineapple
2 yellow grapefruits
1 orange
1 pound head cabbage or Chinese cabbage
1 small cucumber
1 large red bell pepper
2 cups diced, cooked ham

4 tablespoons olive oil
2 tablespoons white wine vinegar
2 tablespoons mayonnaise (see page 99)
2 tablespoons heavy cream
½ teaspoon salt
1 teaspoon sugar

Cut the skin from the pineapple and slice the fruit in half lengthwise. Remove the core and cut the flesh into chunks. Peel the grapefruit, discard the seeds and as much connective tissue and skin as possible, and break the flesh into pieces. Grate the orange rind and reserve it, then peel the orange and break the flesh into pieces. Shred the cabbage, and peel and dice the cucumber. Remove the core and seeds from the red bell pepper and dice it.

In a salad bowl combine the pineapple, grapefruit, orange, cabbage, cucumber, and pepper. Add the ham and toss lightly. Cover and refrigerate.

Mix the grated orange rind with the oil, vinegar, mayonnaise, and cream. Add the salt and sugar and mix well. Taste and adjust the seasoning if necessary. Chill well.

Pour the dressing over the salad just before serving. Makes 8 to 10 servings.

Polish Egg Salad

Citrus: lemon

4 hard-cooked eggs, coarsely chopped
1 large red onion, minced
1 lemon, juice squeezed

2 teaspoons salad oil
½ teaspoon salt
½ teaspoon black pepper
4 tablespoons minced parsley

Mix the eggs with the onion. Add the oil and lemon juice and sprinkle with salt and pepper. Pile into a dish and sprinkle with the parsley. Serve with matzo or black bread. Makes 4 servings.

Grapefruit and Carrot Salad

Citrus: grapefruit

½ head romaine lettuce
1 pound young carrots, split lengthwise
6 yellow grapefruits, peeled and sectioned
2 cups dates, pitted
½ cup walnut halves
1½ cups grapefruit dressing (instructions follow)

Arrange romaine lettuce leaves on six individual salad plates. Arrange the carrot slices and grapefruit sections alternately on the lettuce leaves. Pile a few dates in the center of each plate, and sprinkle the dates with a couple of walnut halves.

Serve with the grapefruit dressing. Makes 6 servings.

GRAPEFRUIT DRESSING:

1 cup salad oil
½ cup grapefruit juice
¼ teaspoon white pepper
½ teaspoon salt
½ teaspoon sugar
1 tablespoon minced fresh mint

Combine all ingredients in a blender and blend until smooth. Makes 1½ cups.

Greek Salad

Citrus: lemon

2 large heads romaine lettuce
2 cucumbers, peeled and diced
4 tomatoes, peeled, seeded, and diced
2 red onions, sliced thin
½ pound Greek (black) olives, pitted
½ pound feta cheese, cubed
1 teaspoon black pepper
1 teaspoon salt
1 tablespoon dried oregano
3 garlic cloves, minced
2 lemons, juice squeezed
1 tablespoon Worcestershire sauce
½ cup olive oil

Tear the lettuce into pieces and toss it with the cucumber, tomatoes, and onions. Cover and chill.

Mix the rest of the ingredients together and chill. Toss the salad and dressing together just before serving. Makes 8 servings.

To toast seeds or nuts, put them in a dry skillet over medium heat and cook, stirring frequently, until they give off their characteristic aroma. This means they are releasing their oils. Remove them from the heat when they are only lightly browned.

Tangelo Turkey Salad
Citrus: tangelo

3 tangelos
3 cups diced cooked turkey
2 celery stalks, chopped
1 cup seedless green grapes
1 teaspoon salt

1 teaspoon curry powder
1 cup mayonnaise
 (see page 99)
5 tablespoons toasted
 sesame seeds

Peel and section the tangelos. Combine them with the turkey, celery, green grapes, and salt. Cover and refrigerate at least 1 hour.

Just before serving, combine the curry powder and the mayonnaise. Add the mixture to the salad, and toss. Sprinkle with sesame seeds. Makes 8 to 10 servings.

Thanks to Mrs. Thelma Nuse, of Caldwell, Kansas, for this recipe.

Molded Citrus Salad
Citrus: orange, lemon

1 envelope unflavored
 gelatin
2 medium oranges
2 tablespoons sugar
1/4 teaspoon salt

1/2 lemon, juice squeezed
1 tablespoon white wine
 vinegar
1/4 head cabbage, shredded
1 celery stalk, chopped fine

Soften the gelatin in 1/2 cup cold water and leave for 15 minutes. Peel one orange, divide it into sections, and remove the skin. Break up the flesh into small chunks, reserving any juice. Squeeze the juice from the other orange.

Pour the gelatin mixture into the top half of a double boiler and stir over medium heat until the gelatin dissolves. Add the orange juice, lemon juice, and vinegar. Remove the pan from the heat, pour the liquid into a bowl, and leave to cool. Refrigerate until the liquid has begun to jell, about 30 minutes. Stir in the rest of the ingredients and pour into a 3 1/2 cup mold. Chill until firm.

Makes 6 servings.

Citrus Artichoke Salad

Citrus: orange, lemon

2 6-ounce jars marinated
    artichoke hearts
1 lemon, juice squeezed
4 garlic cloves, peeled and
    minced
4 oranges

¼ pound small mushrooms,
    sliced
½ teaspoon powdered
    saffron
½ teaspoon salt
½ teaspoon black pepper

Drain the marinade from the artichoke hearts and pour it in a heavy-bottomed saucepan. Add the garlic. Cook 10 minutes, then add the lemon juice, mushrooms, saffron, salt, and pepper. Cover and simmer for 10 minutes over low heat.

Peel 2 of the oranges and section them. Add them to the pan with 1 cup water, bring to a boil, and simmer for 15 minutes.

Pour the mixture into a bowl, add the artichoke hearts, and leave to cool. When cool, cover with plastic wrap and refrigerate for at least 1 hour.

To serve, slice the remaining oranges into rings. Remove the peel and arrange the slices around the edges of 6 individual salad plates. Pile the artichoke mixture into the center of the dishes. Serve chilled. Makes 6 servings.

Kibbutz Carrot Salad

Citrus: orange, tangerine, lemon

2 pounds young carrots,
    grated
2 lemons, juice squeezed
2 tablespoons honey

2 oranges and 1 tangerine
    (or 3 oranges), juice
    squeezed
2 tablespoons brown sugar

Place the grated carrots in salad bowl and pour the citrus juices over them. Add 1 cup water, the sugar, and the honey, and stir well. Cover with plastic wrap and refrigerate for at least 8 hours to allow the flavors to mingle. Serve chilled. Makes 8 servings.

1 large pink grapefruit, peeled and sectioned

2 large oranges, peeled and sectioned

4 bananas, sliced

1 cup pineapple chunks, fresh or canned

1 cup pitted, chopped dates

8 ounces seedless green grapes, sliced in half

1 head butter lettuce

2 kiwi fruit

½ cup shelled pecans

Cooked citrus dressing (instructions follow)

Citrus Fruit Salad with Cooked Citrus Dressing

Citrus: grapefruit, orange, lemon, lime

Toss the grapefruit, orange, bananas, pineapple, dates, and grapes. Chill them thoroughly.

When ready to serve the salad, arrange the lettuce on 8 individual salad plates. Peel the kiwi (dip it in hot water first to loosen the skin), and cut it crosswise into thin slices. Arrange the kiwi slices around the edges of the salad plates, and pile the chilled fruit in the center. Sprinkle with pecans. Serve with cooked citrus dressing. Makes 8 servings.

COOKED CITRUS DRESSING:

1 cup pineapple juice

1 lemon, juice squeezed

1 orange, juice squeezed

2 tablespoons honey

1 tablespoon cornstarch

¼ teaspoon salt

2 eggs, separated

1 cup heavy cream

Combine the fruit juices and stir in the cornstarch and honey. Pour the mixture in a saucepan and bring to a boil, stirring constantly. Boil for 10 minutes.

Remove the pan from the heat, and leave it to cool slightly while you beat the egg yolks. Add the yolks to the sauce, and pour the mixture into the top half of a double boiler. Cook over low heat, stirring constantly, until the mixture is smooth and thick, about 5 minutes.

Remove the pan from the heat. Whip the egg whites into stiff peaks and fold them into the mixture. Leave the mixture to cool. Chill and beat in the cream just before serving. This dressing will keep for up to 1 week, tightly covered, if you do not add the cream until it is to be used. Makes 3 cups.

Indonesian Salad
Citrus: lime, pomelo
or grapefruit

Terasi (or *balachan*, as it is known in Malaya), is a paste made from fermented shrimp. It is available in Oriental food stores, but if you cannot get it, use Marmite or Vegemite (hydrolized yeast paste) or anchovy paste. All of these are available in the gourmet or international foods section of many supermarkets.

Canned bamboo shoots are also available in large supermarkets, as well as in Oriental groceries.

2 small dried hot red peppers
½ cup peanuts
1 tablespoon brown sugar
½ teaspoon terasi
½ teaspoon salt
1 lime, juice squeezed
2 cups shredded Chinese
    cabbage

1 cup sliced bamboo shoots
1 cup bean sprouts
1 pomelo or grapefruit,
    peeled and skinned
2 green onions, minced
2 hard-cooked eggs, coarsely
    chopped
1 tablespoon chili powder

Grind the peppers and peanuts in a blender or food processor. Mix with the brown sugar, terasi, salt, and lime juice.

Combine all the remaining ingredients except the chili powder in a salad bowl. Pour the pepper and peanut mixture over them and toss well. Sprinkle with chili powder before serving. The salad can be decorated with extra green onions and with red bell pepper or pimento strips. Makes 4 to 6 servings.

Green Salad with
Florida Dressing
Citrus: orange

1 large orange, juice
    squeezed
4 tablespoons olive oil
1 teaspoon salt

A combination of any of
the following fresh
greens: spinach, sorrel,
lettuce (any kind), chard,
and Chinese cabbage,
chopped coarsely

Beat the ingredients thoroughly or combine them in a blender. Place greens in a bowl and toss them with the dressing. Makes 6 servings.

1 tablespoon potato starch
  or cornstarch
1 lemon, juice squeezed
1 orange, juice squeezed

3 tablespoons sugar
2 tablespoons butter, cut
  into pieces

Sweet Orange Sauce
Citrus: lemon, orange

Mix the potato starch or cornstarch with 4 tablespoons water. Put the lemon and orange juice in a saucepan, and add 1 cup water and the sugar. Stir over medium heat until the sugar dissolves, then increase the heat and bring to a boil.

Remove the pan from the heat and stir in the potato starch or cornstarch. Return the pan to the heat and stir until the sauce thickens.

Remove the pan from the heat and stir in the butter. Serve hot with puddings, pancakes, ice cream, etc.

Makes 1½ cups.

Hollandaise Sauce
Citrus: lemon

Though it is usually served with asparagus or poached fish, hollandaise sauce is equally good with any kind of steamed or boiled fish or vegetable.

2 tablespoons lemon juice	½ pound (2 sticks) salted
4 large egg yolks	butter, cut into small
	pieces

Fill a bowl with ice water and keep it nearby in case of emergency.

Beat the lemon juice and egg yolks in a metal bowl smaller than the bowl holding the ice water. Stand this bowl over a pan of gently simmering water, making sure it does not touch the surface of the water. Stirring constantly with a wooden spoon, add the pieces of butter, one at a time, waiting until one piece has melted before adding the next. Use a spatula to push the sauce down from the sides of the bowl. Stir until the sauce begins to thicken. If the sauce thickens before all the butter has been stirred in, or if it shows signs of curdling, transfer the bowl immediately to the bowl of ice water, and keep stirring until the sauce thins.

When the sauce is ready, taste for salt and add more if required. Makes 1½ cups.

Lemon Barbecue Sauce
Citrus: lemon

Creole spice is a milder chili powder from New Orleans. It is available in gourmet shops.

2 garlic cloves	1 teaspoon dried thyme
½ teaspoon salt	1 teaspoon dried chervil
½ teaspoon chili powder	8 tablespoons olive oil
or Creole spice	4 lemons, juice squeezed
1 teaspoon oregano	and strained

Pound the garlic and salt together in a bowl. Stir in the rest of the ingredients. Cover and leave for at least 24 hours before using as a marinade for broiled meat or poultry. Very good with lamb.

Makes 1 cup.

To make herb butter, chop 6 sprigs of fresh coriander (cilantro) or tarragon with the parsley. When using this butter with steak, you might add minced shallot or 2 minced garlic cloves.

Maitre d'Hôtel Butter
Citrus: lemon

¼ pound (1 stick) sweet
  butter, softened

6 sprigs parsley, chopped
  fine
½ lemon, juice squeezed

Beat the ingredients thoroughly until well combined. Shape the butter into a block or individual pats. Wrap in wax paper and chill until required, but no more than 24 hours.

Put a lump or pat of the butter on top of broiled fish or steak.

Makes ½ cup.

This is the simplest sauce to make in the whole world if you have a blender. Extra spices and herbs can be added with the egg and lemon to suit your taste. I often add parsley, grated citrus rind, and minced garlic. If you add chopped pickles and chopped hard-cooked eggs, the sauce gets a new name—it becomes remoulade sauce. Chopped pickles, olives, and horseradish will turn it into tartar sauce. I prefer a thick mayonnaise, but if you want a thinner one, stir in some more lemon juice by hand just before using.

Mayonnaise
Citrus: lemon

1 large egg
1 large lemon, juice
  squeezed

1 teaspoon dry mustard
½ teaspoon salt
1¼ cups salad oil

Put the egg, lemon juice, dry mustard, and salt in blender and mix until smooth.

With the blender running, begin to add the oil very gradually. Continue to pour in the oil in a thin stream until it is absorbed and the mixture thickens.

Transfer the mayonnaise to a bottle or jar. Close the jar tightly but do not seal it. Store in the refrigerator. The mayonnaise will keep for about 1 week.

Makes 1½ cups.

Sauce Diable
(Mustard and
Lemon Sauce)
Citrus: lemon

2 lemons, juice squeezed
8 tablespoons olive oil
½ teaspoon salt

½ teaspoon white pepper
1 teaspoon dry mustard
2 garlic cloves, minced

Pour all the ingredients into a bowl or blender and combine thoroughly. Serve with broiled fish or game.
Makes 1 cup.

Sauce Maltaise
(Maltese Sauce)
Citrus: blood orange

This sauce is so named because the best blood oranges were once grown in Malta. The sauce is a variation on hollandaise, and it is used in the same way.

2 blood oranges
2 tablespoons lemon juice
½ teaspoon salt
½ teaspoon white pepper

3 egg yolks, well beaten
6 ounces (1½ sticks) butter,
    softened and cut into
    tiny pieces

Squeeze the juice from the blood oranges and strain it. Grate ½ teaspoon of rind from one orange. Reserve the juice and grated rind.

In the top half of a double boiler placed over direct heat, boil the lemon juice with the salt and pepper until the liquid is reduced to a teaspoonful. Simmer the water in the bottom half very gently, and add 1 tablespoon cold water to the liquid in the top half. Beat in the egg yolks and 2 tablespoons of the butter, and continue beating the sauce with a wire whisk until it begins to thicken. Add the rest of the butter in very small quanities, waiting for one piece to melt before adding the next. Between additions of butter add 2 or more tablespoons of cold water, one tablespoon at a time. The water will prevent the sauce from heating too quickly and curdling.

When all the butter has been incorporated, stir in the reserved orange juice and rind. Continue stirring and beating for a few moments to let the sauce warm through and thickens again. Serve warm.
Makes 1½ cups.

This classic English sauce for venison or hare is also popular in Germany.

If bitter oranges are not available, use a sweet orange. Grate the orange and lemon rinds into the finished sauce instead of cutting them into thin strips and parboiling them.

Red currant jelly is available in the gourmet sections of supermarkets.

1 lemon, juice squeezed, rind peeled	½ cup red currant jelly
	½ cup port wine
1 bitter orange, juice squeezed, rind peeled	½ teaspoon ground ginger
	½ teaspoon black pepper

Slice the orange and lemon rinds into very thin strips. Bring a large pan of water to a boil and drop them in. Boil for 5 minutes, then drain. Rinse the strips under cold water, and repeat.

Melt the jelly in a saucepan and add the port wine, spices, and the citrus juice. Boil the sauce over a high heat until it has a syrupy consistency. Add the strips of rind. Serve hot.

Makes about 1¼ cups.

This sauce can be used as a salad dressing or as an ingredient in molded salads. It is delicious, quick and easy to make, and wonderful with cold fish or vegetables. You can add minced herbs if you like.

1 large lemon, juice squeezed and strained	½ teaspoon white pepper
1 teaspoon salt	1 cup heavy or whipping cream

Season the lemon juice with the salt and pepper. Stir until the salt has dissolved. Use a wire whisk to beat in the cream very gradually. Use immediately.

Makes 1¾ cups.

Sauce Bigarade (French Bitter Orange Sauce)
Citrus: bitter orange

This classic sauce for French duck with orange sauce is also very good with pork, ham, and game. When it is served with duck, the cooking juices referred to in the recipe should come from the braised or broiled bird.

2 bitter oranges
1 tablespoon butter
1 tablespoon all-purpose flour

1 cup cooking juices or broth
2 tablespoon sugar

Squeeze the juice from the oranges and strain it. Peel the rind and cut it into narrow strips. Put the strips in a pan of cold water and bring the water to a boil. Drain the rinds, rinse them under cold water, and repeat the process.

Melt the butter in a saucepan. Stir in the flour and cook, stirring, for 3 minutes. Add the cooking juices or broth, the orange juice, and the sugar. Cook, stirring constantly, until the sauce boils. Reduce the heat and simmer for 10 minutes or until it thickens. Add the orange rinds, and serve hot in a sauceboat to be handed with the meat.

Makes 1 cup.

Lime Sauce
Citrus: lime

4 limes
6 tablespoons white rum or triple sec

6 tablespoons sugar
3 drops green food coloring (optional)

Use a potato peeler to peel the limes in very thin strips. Squeeze and reserve the juice.

Put the sugar in a pan with 2 cups water and stir over medium heat until the sugar dissolves. Bring to a boil, and boil without stirring until a drop of the syrup forms a soft ball when dropped in ice water (or until the syrup registers 236° F. on a candy thermometer).

Remove the pan from the heat and stir in the lime juice and rum or triple sec. Serve with hot desserts.

Makes 2 cups.

Citric acid or sour salt, also known as lemon salt, can sometimes be found in the spice section of supermarkets. Jewish delis and Middle Eastern food stores also stock it.

Lime Syrup
Citrus: lime

6 limes, juice squeezed	1 teaspoon sour salt (citric
2 cups sugar	acid)
2 tablespoons white corn	5 drops green coloring
syrup	(optional)

Pour the juice into a saucepan and add the sugar and corn syrup. Stir over medium heat until the sugar has displayed. Brush down any crystals that form on the sides of the pan with a pastry brush dipped in cold water. Bring the liquid to a boil. Boil 5 minutes, then stir in the sour salt and boil 5 minutes more. Remove the pan from the heat. Add the coloring if desired.

Cool to room temperature, then pour into bottles and store in the refrigerator. Use as a sauce for hot or cold desserts, diluted with water or soda as a cold drink, or as flavoring for milk shakes. Makes 2 cups.

Almond meal, made from almonds ground with or without the skins, can be bought at health food stores. I prefer the skinless kind, but either can be used here. You can make your own almond meal by grinding 48 blanched almonds in a food processor or blender. Make sure all the utensils are absolutely moisture-free.

Special Cranberry Sauce
Citrus: tangerine or tangelo

6 tangerines or tangelos	1 pound fresh cranberries
2 cups sugar	2 cups almond meal

Peel the tangerines or tangelos. Remove the seeds, if any, and put the pulp and juice in a blender or food processor. Purée.

Put the sugar in a heavy pan with 1 cup water. Cook, stirring, until the sugar dissolves, then stop stirring and bring the syrup to the boil. Boil briskly for 5 minutes. Add the cranberries, reduce the heat, and return to a boil. Boil for 5 minutes or until the cranberries are transparent. Add the tangerine or tangelo purée and reheat, but do not boil.

Remove the pan from the heat and leave the sauce to cool. When it is cold, stir in the almond meal. Serve the sauce well chilled with turkey, ham, pork, or game. It will keep in refrigerator for 2 weeks. Makes 5 cups.

Orange Mustard Sauce
Citrus: orange or bitter orange

1 cup sweet or bitter orange marmalade
2 oranges, juice squeezed
½ cup cider vinegar
1 cup brown sugar, packed

2 tablespoons dark corn syrup
2 tablespoons Dijon-style mustard

Put all the ingredients in a saucepan and stir over medium heat until the liquid boils. Reduce the heat and cook, stirring occasionally to prevent sticking, for 20 minutes or until well reduced. Use as a basting sauce for barbecued ribs or baked ham, duck, or turkey. Makes about 1½ cups.

Simple Egg and Lemon Sauce
Citrus: lemon

This sauce for boiled fish or chicken will transform a bland dish into a really delicious meal. It also offers the advantage of being easier and less expensive to make than hollandaise sauce.

2 lemons, juice squeezed and strained
2 eggs

1 tablespoon cornstarch or potato starch
2 cups fish or chicken broth

Mix the lemon juice with the cornstarch or potato starch.

Heat the broth. When it is hot but not boiling, stir in the starch mixture. Bring to a boil, stirring constantly over medium heat. Reduce the heat when the liquid boils; simmer 5 minutes.

Remove the pan from the heat and leave it to cool for 15 minutes. Beat the eggs thoroughly and pour the hot liquid over them, beating constantly.

Partly fill the bottom half of a double boiler with water, and pour the sauce into the top half. Return the pan to the stove and simmer over a gentle heat, stirring constantly, until the sauce thickens. Do not let it boil or it will curdle.

Makes 2 cups.

For the same reason fresh citrus keeps so well, it is also excellent for preserving: all the fruits are rich in acid and sugar, the most important natural preservatives.

Many of the recipes in this chapter require canning. If you have never canned foods before, you will find it is much easier than you think, and does not require elaborate equipment. All you need is a heavy-bottomed pan like the ones used in making candy (see "Desserts") and a number of mason jars (Kerr or Ball) in various sizes, plus screw bands and flat lids with rubber seals. You can use other methods of sealing jars, such as with paraffin wax, but they are more time-consuming. All the items you need (except the pan, which can be bought at a good cookware shop or in the cookware department of a department store) should be available at your local supermarket, particularly in the autumn, when preserving is at its height. If you carefully follow the instructions included with the jars and lids, you cannot go wrong. If the manufacturers' directions contradict mine in any of the following recipes, do what they say; they know their product best.

Pickled Mandarins
Citrus: mandarin

Clementines, Wilkins, and Naartjes are all suitable for pickling, but thin-skinned fruit such as Honey mandarins are even better.

18 mandarins
1 cinnamon stick
15 whole cloves
10 allspice berries

1 tablespoon freshly grated
 ginger root
2 cups white wine vinegar
6 tablespoons brown sugar

Prick each mandarin with a needle in several places. Tie all the spices in a piece of cheesecloth. Pour the vinegar into a pan and add the spices and sugar. Bring to a boil. Add the fruit and reduce the heat. Boil over medium-low heat for 20 minutes or until the fruit is soft.

Remove the fruit with a skimmer and distribute it among 3 sterile preserving jars. Boil the vinegar with the spices over high heat until it is reduced by about one fourth, about 30 minutes. Remove and discard the bag of spices, and pour the liquid over the fruits. Seal the jars, and store them in a cool, dark place. Serve with pork or game. Makes about 3 pints.

Kumquat Preserves
Citrus: kumquats

2 pounds kumquats
1¾ cups sugar

¾ cup clear honey

Cut a small cross in each kumquat at the end opposite the stem.

Put the sugar and honey in a heavy-based pan and add 3⅓ cups water. Stir until the sugar dissolves, then bring the liquid to a boil, without stirring, over medium-high heat.

Add the kumquats, reduce the heat, and cook at a slow boil for 1 hour, or until the fruits are translucent. Leave the contents of the pan to cool 15 minutes before bottling in sterile preserving jars.

This preserve, like the tangerine preserve, is wonderful as a sauce for vanilla ice cream or as a topping for yellow cake. Makes about 3 pints.

This is one of the first recipes ever written for lemons. It comes from the pen of Ibn Jamiya, of Cairo, who was Saladin's personal physician. In his twelfth-century treatise on the lemon, this learned doctor recommends storing the pickles in a cool, dark place for forty days, "but if you wait still longer . . . their taste and fragrance will be still more delicious."

Pickled Lemons in Brine
Citrus: lemon

8 lemons
1 cup coarse salt
2 bay leaves

10 allspice berries
10 coriander seeds

Cut 4 of the lemons lengthwise in quarters, leaving them joined by about ½ inch at the end opposite the stem. Open out the cut sides and pack some of the salt between the sections. Squeeze the lemons back into shape.

Sprinkle half the remaining salt in the bottom of a 1-pint jelly jar or any jar with a tight-fitting lid. Pack the lemons tightly, pushing them down firmly so they release their juices. Sprinkle the lemons with extra salt and push the bay leaves down between the lemons. Sprinkle with the allspice berries and coriander seeds.

Squeeze the remaining lemons and strain the juice. Pour it into the jar so that it completely covers the salted lemons. Seal the jar and leave it in the sun for 2 weeks, turning it once a day if possible. Store in a cool, dry place. The lemons will keep for a year unopened. When opened, refrigerate.

To use the lemons, wash them thoroughly to remove excess salt and discard the pulp, using the rinds only. Recipes using pickled lemons can be found under "Meat."

Makes 4 pickled lemons.

Lemon Mincemeat
Citrus: lemon

8 lemons
2 cups sugar
4½ cups (1 pound) raisins

2 cups cold suet or
  cold butter
1 cup brandy

Peel the lemon rinds in very thin strips with a potato peeler. Fill a large pan with water, bring to a boil, and add the rinds. Boil until the rinds are very soft, about 30 minutes. Drain, discarding the water.

Beat the sugar and lemon rinds together until the rinds are impregnated with sugar. Shred or chop the suet or butter in very small pieces. Combine the sugared rinds with the raisins and fat.

Squeeze the juice from four of the lemons and stir it into the mixture. Transfer the mixture to sterile preserving jars. Seal, and store in a cool, dark place. The mixture will keep for about a year.

Serve with ham or poultry. Traditionally eaten as a pie or cookie filling at Christmas time.

Makes 1½ pints.

Fresh Cranberry Relish
Citrus: orange

2 large oranges
4 cups (1 pound) fresh
  cranberries

2 red apples
2 cups honey or maple syrup

Peel the oranges, reserving half the rind from one. Cut away as much of the pith from the rind as possible, and grate the rind coarsely. Chop the cranberries coarsely. Quarter and core the apples but do not peel them. Chop them coarsely with the orange flesh.

Combine the cranberries, apples, and orange flesh. Put the mixture in a bowl, and add the shredded rind and honey or syrup. Leave at room temperature for 2 weeks, covered with a cloth, to allow the flavors to blend. Transfer to jelly jars; close tightly but do not seal. Refrigerate for at least 1 day before eating. Since this relish is uncooked, it must be stored in the refrigerator and will keep for only 2 weeks.

Makes about 1 quart.

4 large pink grapefruit
2 cups sugar
1 lemon
1 orange

1½ cups fresh berries
(strawberries, raspberries,
ollalieberries, boysen-
berries, etc.)

Grapefruit-Berry Relish

Citrus: grapefruit, lemon, orange

Peel the grapefruit and discard the peel, the pith, and as much of the skin covering the segments as possible.

Put the grapefruit, berries, and sugar in a heavy pan and cook over low heat, stirring with a wooden spoon until the sugar dissolves.

Strain the mixture through a sieve. Transfer the liquid to another pan and boil it rapidly without stirring until it thickens to a syrupy consistency, about 15 minutes. Add the strained fruit to the syrup.

Grate the rinds of the lemon and orange and squeeze the juice from the lemon. Strain the juice and add it to the mixture with the citrus rinds. Bring the mixture back to a boil, and boil 10 minutes. Cool to room temperature, then pour into jars, cover, and refrigerate. Wait at least 24 hours before using; it will keep about 1 month in the refrigerator. Delicious with cold meats and salads.

Makes 3 cups.

This Victorian recipe is taken from Mrs. Esther Levy's *Jewish Cookery Book*, the first Jewish cookbook ever published in the United States. Fresh horseradish is always obtainable around Easter, since it is used by Jews for the Passover meal.

Limequats or calamondins may be substituted for the lemons or limes.

Lemon or Lime Relish

Citrus: lemon or lime

6 lemons or limes, juice
squeezed and strained
2 tablespoons grated
horseradish
2 tablespoons ground ginger
or 4 tablespoons grated
ginger root

1 tablespoon grated nutmeg
1 tablespoon ground
cinnamon
2 cups white vinegar

Pour the lemon or lime juice in a pan and add the rest of the ingredients. Bring to a boil, and boil briskly for 10 minutes. Strain and bottle. Store in a cool, dry place. Makes 1 pint.

Green Lime Chutney
Citrus: lime

This condiment is not as chunky as most Indian chutneys. It is typical of the Bengal region.

4 cups (1 bunch) coriander
(cilantro) leaves
1 cup (6 sprigs) fresh mint
leaves
1 tablespoon brown sugar

2 small hot green chilies,
seeded and chopped
1 lime, juice squeezed
and strained
1 teaspoon salt

Grind the coriander and mint leaves in a food mill or blender, or mince them by hand. Add the rest of the ingredients and blend until smooth. Store in spice jars, and use to season stews and curries.

Makes about 1 cup.

Lime or Calamondin Marmalade
Citrus: lime or calamondin

Limequats or Rangpur limes may be substituted for the limes or calamondins in this recipe.

2 pounds limes or
calamondins

4 pounds (8 cups) sugar

Wash the fruit and put it in a large pan with water to cover. Bring 2½ quarts water to a boil and cover the pan tightly. Simmer the limes for about 2 hours, or until they are very tender and are easily pierced with a toothpick.

Remove the limes from the pan, reserving the water. Cut the fruits in thin slices, taking care not to waste the juice, and reserve the seeds, if any. Return the fruit to the pan. Put the seeds in a piece of cheesecloth and tie it securely.

Add the sugar to the pan. Stir with a wooden spoon over gentle heat until the sugar dissolves. Increase the heat and bring the contents of the pan to a boil. Boil rapidly for about 45 minutes or until the setting point is reached (220° F. on a candy thermometer). Discard the bag of seeds. Remove the pan from the heat and leave it to stand for about 15 minutes. Then bottle the marmalade in sterile preserving jars and seal. Makes about 7 pints.

5 lemons
6 artichoke bottoms, cooked
2 cups cauliflower florets
6 carrots, sliced in thin
   rounds

2 cups green or yellow
   snap beans
4 tablespoons coarse salt
About 2 cups olive oil

Macedoine de Legumes Confits (Lemon and Mixed Vegetable Pickle)

Citrus: lemon

Cut 3 of the lemons in thin slices. Arrange the slices in a large colander, and place the colander over a large crock. Mix the rest of the vegetables in a bowl, then transfer them to the colander and sprinkle them with the salt. Stir to distribute the salt evenly.

Leave the bowl in a cool, dark place (not the refrigerator) for 24 hours. Discard the brine that has drained into the crock.

Arrange the vegetables in sterile preserving jars. Squeeze the juice from the remaining lemons and distribute it evenly among the jars. Pour olive oil over the vegetables, making sure that all the spaces between them are filled. Seal the jars and store them in a cool, dark place. Turn them occasionally to distribute the liquid evenly. Do not open for at least 3 weeks. Refrigerate after opening.

Makes about 3 pints.

Dried Citrus Peel

Drying concentrates the aromatic oils in citrus peel. For this recipe use only thin-skinned fruit of such aromatic varieties as the bitter orange, tangerine, lime, and lemon, or peel the rind in a thin layer from thick-skinned fruit. Use the dried peel—whole (remove the peel before serving), or ground in a spice grinder—instead of freshly grated peel to flavor stewed fruits and soup.

6 citrus fruits

Score the peel in quarters and remove it, or peel the fruit in long strips. Dry the peels in an oven on its lowest setting for 6 hours, or leave them in the hot sun for 2 days. Put the peels in a tightly closed container, such as a spice jar. Store in a dark, cool, dry place; do not refrigerate.

Makes between 4 and 8 tablespoons when ground.

A Very Superior Mincemeat

Citrus: lemon, citron, orange

"A Very Superior Mincemeat" is the title under which this recipe appears in an old English cookbook, and it certainly lives up to its name. If you cannot find suet (beef kidney fat), you can use lard or butter, but the fat must have the hard, smooth consistency that permits it to be chopped. Mace is sometimes hard to find in the United States; if you can't get it, substitute extra nutmeg. Candied oranges can be bought at gourmet stores (or make your own; see the recipe on page 131).

3 lemons
1 pound apples
½ pound cooked beef
   tongue, chopped
1 cup (½ pound) suet,
   chopped
3 cups (1 pound) raisins,
   chopped
3 cups (1 pound) currants,
   chopped
1¼ cups sugar

4 ounces candied citron,
   chopped
4 ounces candied orange,
   chopped
1 whole nutmeg, grated
½ teaspoon salt
½ teaspoon ground mace
1 teaspoon freshly grated
   ginger root
⅔ cup brandy
⅔ cup sweet sherry

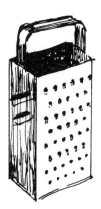

Put 2 whole lemons in water to cover, and boil briskly for 20 minutes or until the peel can be pierced easily with a toothpick. Remove the lemons and drain them. Cut them in half and remove any seeds. Grind the lemons in a blender or food processor. Grate the rind of the other lemon, and squeeze the juice from it.

Peel and core the apples and chop them fine. Sprinkle the chopped apple with the lemon juice.

Put all the ingredients except the liquor in a grinder or food processor and mince or grind them together. Add the brandy and sherry and stir well. Press the mincemeat into sterile preserving jars and seal. Store in a cool, dark place. The mincemeat will keep, unopened, for about 1 year.

Makes about 5 pints.

Thanks to the Food and Drug Administration, the makers of my store-bought lemon pepper have been forced to reveal on the label that the main ingredient of their product is salt, followed (of course) by monosodium glutamate and the ubiquitous sugar. Other similar commercial spice mixtures contain, in addition to the above ingredients, modified corn starch, "artificial flavorings," and yellow dye number 5. The following recipe, besides omitting the sinister ingredients in the store-bought condiment, has the virtue of being salt- and sugar-free. You may have to invest in a spice grinder, but that is a small price to pay.

Salt-free Lemon Spice
Citrus: lemon

Citric acid, or sour salt, is sometimes available in the spice sections of supermarkets, and can also be bought in Middle Eastern and Jewish groceries. It is also known as lemon salt.

1 tablespoon ground dried
  lemon peel
1 tablespoon ground allspice

½ tablespoon sour salt
  (citric acid)

Grind the citrus peel in a spice or coffee grinder. Put all the ingredients into a spice jar, seal tightly, and shake well to mix. Use to season meat and vegetable dishes.
    Makes 2½ tablespoons.

Special Citrus Jelly
Citrus: orange, lemon

1 orange, juice squeezed
1 lemon, juice squeezed
1½ cups dry red wine

3 cups sugar
2 tablespoons triple sec or
  Grand Marnier liqueur

Warm the sugar by putting it in a cake pan and leaving it for 15 minutes in an oven preheated to its lowest setting.
    Strain the juice of the orange and lemon through several layers of cheesecloth. Put the seeds in a cheesecloth bag.
    Put the juices and wine in a pan and bring them to a boil. Add the sugar and the bag of seeds, and boil for 10 minutes. Add the liqueur and cook another 5 minutes. Remove the cheesecloth bag. Pour into sterile preserving jars and seal. Makes about 1 quart.

Grapefruit Mint Jelly

Citrus: grapefruit

Use yellow grapefruit in this recipe for the best color.

To test whether a jelly is ready to bottle, pour 1 teaspoon of the liquid in a bowl and add 2 tablespoons of pure alcohol, such as rubbing alcohol. If it forms a large clot, the jelly is ready for bottling. If the clots are small and scattered, continue boiling.

3 large grapefruit	3½ cups sugar
1 bunch (about 2 ounces) fresh mint, chopped fine	3 drops green coloring (optional)

Warm the sugar in a cake pan for 15 minutes in an oven preheated to its lowest setting.

Peel the rind from the grapefruit with a potato peeler. Discard the rind or dry it for other uses (see page 111). Squeeze the juice from the fruit, and reserve the seeds and all the pith and pulp. Tie the pith and seeds in a cheesecloth bag.

Strain the juice through 2 or 3 layers of cheesecloth, and measure it into a preserving pan. You should have at least 2¼ cups; if not, add more strained juice from another grapefruit. Add ¾ cup water, the sugar, and the bag containing the grapefruit pulp. Stir until the sugar dissolves, then increase the heat and boil for 20 minutes or until the liquid jells when tested. Stir in the mint and remove the pan from the heat. Add coloring, if desired, and pour into sterile preserving jars. Seal tightly. Refrigerate after opening. Traditionally eaten with roast lamb, but good with cold ham as well.

Makes about 1 quart.

This classic preserve is said to have originated when a cask of Seville oranges was lost at sea and washed up on the coast of Dundee, Scotland. Sea water had leaked into the barrel, partially pickling the oranges. The thrifty Scots, not wishing to waste the precious fruit, decided to preserve it.

Although very good marmalades are made with other citrus, only sour or bitter fruits have the tanginess that distinguishes marmalade from jam and jelly.

Bitter Orange Marmalade

Citrus: bitter orange, lemon

2 pounds bitter oranges	4 pounds (8 cups) sugar
2 lemons	4 tablespoons scotch whisky

Cut the fruit into quarters. Remove the seeds and reserve them. Scrape the pulp from the skins and reserve it. Put the peel in cold water to cover. Tie the seeds in a piece of cheesecloth and soak them with the peel for 24 hours.

Drain the peel and seeds. Shred the peel, coarse or fine according to taste. Put the cheesecloth bag and the shredded peel in a preserving pan, and cover with 2 quarts water. Boil, covered, over medium heat for 1 hour. Remove the bag of seeds.

Warm the sugar by putting it in a cake pan and leaving it for 15 minutes in an oven preheated to its lowest setting. Purée the fruit pulp, and add it with the sugar to the pan of shredded peel. Stir over low heat until the sugar has dissolved, then increase the heat slightly and bring to a boil. Without stirring, boil about 45 minutes until the marmalade sets (or until it reaches 220° F. on a candy thermometer).

Remove the pan from the heat and stir in the whisky immediately. Bottle in sterile preserving jars while still hot. Seal tightly. Improves with age.

Makes about 3½ pints.

Lemon Marmalade
Citrus: lemon

About 2 pounds (4 cups) sugar

6 lemons

Weigh the fruit. For every pound of fruit, use two pounds of sugar.

Put the whole fruit into a saucepan, and add 6 cups water. Boil for 2 hours, covered. Drain the fruit, discarding the water. Bring 6 cups water to a boil and pour it over the fruit. Leave the lemons in the water until cool. Drain and discard the water.

Cut the lemons in thin slices, removing the seeds. Weigh the fruit and reserve it.

Warm the sugar by putting it in a cake pan and leaving it for 15 minutes in an oven preheated to its lowest setting. Put the sugar in a preserving pan, and add 1¼ cups water to every pound of sugar. Stir over low heat with a wooden spoon until the sugar has completely dissolved. Add the fruit, and boil over a brisk heat for 45 minutes or until it jells when tested. Remove from the heat; bottle in sterile preserving jars and seal. Makes about 5 pints.

Citron or Pomelo Marmalade
Citrus: citron, pomelo

Citrons may also be preserved as candy; see "Desserts."

1 large or 4 small (Etrog) citrons, or 2 pomelos (about 4 pounds)

About 4 pounds (8 cups) sugar

Cut the fruit in quarters lengthwise. Scoop out the pulp and seeds, and tie them in cheesecloth. Soak the peel, pulp, and seeds in water overnight. Drain.

Weigh the fruit. Put it in a preserving pan and add an equal weight of sugar. Add water to cover. Stir over low heat until the sugar has dissolved. Add the cheesecloth bag containing the pulp and seeds. Increase the heat and cook for 45 minutes, or until the marmalade jells when tested. Bottle in sterile preserving jars and seal while hot.

Makes about 6 pints.

Any combination of citrus fruit can be used in this recipe, as long as the total weight of the raw fruit is half that of the sugar.

Five-Fruit Marmalade

Citrus: grapefruit, lemon, lime, bitter orange, tangerine

2 grapefruit
2 lemons
2 limes
2 bitter oranges

2 tangerines
About 6 pounds (12 cups) sugar

Quarter the fruit. Peel the rinds in thin strips with a potato peeler. Cut the peeled fruit into quarters. Remove and reserve the seeds. Peel off the pith and put it with the seeds, cores, connective tissue, and the skin covering the grapefruit segments in a cheesecloth bag.

Put the rinds, pulp, and cheesecloth bag in a large bowl, and add 7½ pints cold water. Leave for at least 24 hours.

Put the contents of the bowl in a preserving pan. Bring to a boil and simmer on very low heat until the rinds are very soft, about 2 hours.

Remove the pan from the heat. Take out the cheesecloth bag and suspend it over the pan until most of the liquid has dripped out of it, but do not squeeze it. Discard the bag.

Return the pan to the heat and bring the liquid to a boil. Add the sugar, and remove the pan from the heat again. Stir with a wooden spoon until the sugar has dissolved. Return the pan to the heat and boil rapidly, without stirring, until the marmalade sets when tested, about 45 minutes.

Remove the pan from the heat and let it stand 15 minutes. Bottle the marmalade in sterile preserving jars and seal. Makes about 9 pints.

Kumquat and Carrot Marmalade
Citrus: kumquat

An excellent way of using up overripe kumquats.

8 cups kumquats	1 cinnamon stick
6 large carrots, grated	About 6 cups sugar

Cut the kumquats in half and remove as many seeds as you can (the very small ones are hard to spot). Grind the fruits fairly coarsely. Transfer the kumquats and any juice to a heavy-based pan, and add 1 cup water. Bring to a boil and cook, uncovered, until the fruit is tender, about 15 minutes. Add the carrots and cook another 5 minutes.

Measure the mixture and add an equal amount of sugar. Add the cinnamon stick. Cook over low heat, stirring until the sugar dissolves. Bring to a boil over low heat and cook until the syrup is thick, about 45 minutes. Stir frequently to prevent burning, and skim off any foam and seeds that rise to the surface.

Remove the pan from the heat, and discard the cinnamon stick. Wait 15 minutes before bottling the marmalade in sterile preserving jars, then seal. Makes about 3 quarts.

Greek Citrus Blossom Preserves
Citrus: lemon

Any citrus blossom will do for this recipe. The Greeks usually use lemons, but the blossom of bitter oranges and grapefruit are even more fragrant.

1 pound citrus blossom	1 lemon, juice squeezed
3 pounds (6 cups) sugar	and strained

Mix the blossom with 2 tablespoons of the sugar and leave in a bowl overnight, covered, at room temperature.

The next day, put the rest of the sugar in a heavy-based pan and heat it over a gentle heat until it is warmed through. Add 2½ cups water and the lemon juice and cook, stirring, until the sugar dissoves. Boil without stirring for 5 minutes. Add the lemon blossom and cook for 30 minutes over medium heat, or until the blossom is transparent and the liquid is syrupy. Bottle in sterilized preserving jars while hot, but do not seal until cool. The syrup should be the consistency of clear honey. Makes about 4 pints.

This delicious preserve is served in Greece and the Middle East as an accompaniment to Turkish coffee. A glass of ice water is served on the side.

Naringue (Bitter Orange Peel Preserves)

Citrus: bitter orange, lemon

8 pounds bitter oranges
2 pounds (4 cups) sugar
1 lemon, juice squeezed

4 tablespoons light corn syrup

Use a potato peeler to remove the orange rind in strips as long and thin as possible. Soak the rind in water to cover with a handful of coarse salt, changing the water daily, for 3 days.

Put the rind in a heavy-based pan and add water to cover. Boil the rind, covered, for 30 minutes, or until a toothpick pierces it easily. Remove the rind from the pan and drain it thoroughly. Leave it to cool.

Roll up each strip of rind into a tight coil. Thread a darning needle with nylon thread. Thread the coils together in a string. Knot the ends of the thread together.

Boil the sugar with 3 cups water and the corn syrup, stirring until the sugar dissolves. Add the lemon juice, and bring to a boil without stirring. Boil 5 minutes, then add the string of orange rind coils. Simmer over a low heat, uncovered, for 1 hour.

Remove the string of coils and lay it on wax paper to drain and cool. When cool enough to handle, cut the thread and discard it. Put four or five coils in each of ten sterile one-pint preserving jars.

Boil the syrup again for 15 minutes or until it is the consistency of clear honey. Cool it slightly, then pour it over the orange rind coils. The coils must be completely covered with syrup. Seal the jars. Serve the peels in syrup, or leave them to dry and roll them in confectioner's sugar like a candy.

Makes 10 pints.

Tangerine Preserves
Citrus: tangerine

Choose very sweet tangerines, or substitute very sweet tangelos or tangors.

3 pounds tangerines   3 pounds (6 cups) sugar

Cut the tangerines in half and scoop out the pulp. Discard the seeds. Purée the pulp in a blender or food processor and set it aside.

Shred the tangerine peel coarsely with a knife or in a food processor. Bring a large pan of boiling water to a boil, and throw in the peel. Bring the water back to a boil, and boil for 5 minutes. Drain, and discard the water. Fill the pan with fresh water and bring it to a boil again. Add the peels and boil again for 5 minutes. Repeat the process twice more.

Pour the puréed pulp into a preserving pan. Add the sugar and the peel. Cook, stirring until the sugar has dissolved, then bring to a boil without stirring for 30 minutes or until the liquid sets when tested. Remove the pan from the heat and leave for 15 minutes. Seal in sterile preserving jars. Makes about 5 pints.

1 stick butter, softened
½ cup brown sugar
3 eggs, separated
1 cup ground walnuts
⅔ cup all-purpose flour,
  sifted

1 large mandarin, juice
  squeezed, rind grated
½ cup chocolate chips
¼ cup sugar

Chocolate Chip Mandarin Cake

Citrus: mandarin

Grease an 8-inch square cake pan. Preheat the oven to 375° F.

Beat the butter with the brown sugar until smooth. Beat in the egg yolks, ground nuts, flour, and mandarin juice and rind. Stir in the chocolate chips.

Whip the egg whites with the sugar into stiff peaks. Fold them into the mixture. Transfer the mixture to the pan, and bake 40 minutes or until a knife inserted in the center of the cake comes out clean. Cut into squares to serve. Makes 16 2-inch squares.

Sussex Pond Pudding
Citrus: lemon

This traditional English pudding is often served at ceremonial banquets given by the Lord Mayor of London. The "pond" comes from the delicious puddle of brown sugar and lemon juice that forms under the crust. The suet can be replaced by ice-cold butter.

2 lemons	½ cup skimmed milk
½ cup all-purpose flour	½ cup raisins
½ teaspoon baking powder	1 stick butter, cut into pieces
6 tablespoons suet	3 tablespoons brown sugar

Bring a large pan of water to a boil and drop in the whole lemons. Cook them until their skins are tender enough to be pierced with a skewer, about 30 minutes. Heavily grease a 1-quart metal bowl or pudding basin.

Sift the flour and baking powder and combine them with the suet, in an electric mixer or food processor or by hand. Add just enough skimmed milk to make a smooth, soft dough. Add the raisins to the dough and mix. Roll the dough into a ball, and divide it into two pieces, one twice as large as the other.

Roll the larger piece of dough into a circle and use it to line the pudding basin. Dot the dough with half the pieces of butter. Sprinkle it with half the sugar.

Cut the lemons into 4 slices attached at one end, and set them in the pudding basin vertically. Sprinkle them with the rest of the sugar and dot them with the rest of the butter. Roll out the reserved dough and lay it on top of the lemon, sealing the edges of the two pieces of dough firmly.

Cut a circle of aluminum foil at least 2 inches larger in diameter than the top of the basin. Tie it securely over the basin to make a lid, leaving a strong loop of string by which to pull the basin from the cooking water (if your basin has a tight-fitting plastic lid, use that instead).

Put the pudding basin in a large pan of boiling water. The water should reach about halfway up the basin. Simmer the pudding over low heat for 2 hours, adding more water when necessary.

Unmold the pudding on a serving dish, and cut it so everyone gets a piece of lemon. Serve it with or without custard. Makes 6 servings.

When using a sugar thermometer, always warm it in hot water before dipping it in hot syrup.

Lime and Coconut Pudding

Citrus: lime

2 tablespoons golden raisins
1 lime, juice squeezed, rind grated
4 cups unsweetened shredded coconut, or 1 cup fresh coconut milk and 1 cup fresh grated coconut

1½ cups sugar
5 whole cloves tied in cheesecloth
2 egg yolks
2 tablespoons white rum (optional)

Soak the raisins in the lime juice for at least 10 minutes.

If you are able to use fresh coconut, extract the milk by grating half of a fresh coconut into a bowl, adding 1 pint water, and squeezing handfuls of the coconut in the water. Strain the liquid and discard the squeezed coconut. Grate the other half of the coconut and reserve it.

If you are using dried coconut, boil it in 1 cup water for 5 minutes. Strain the liquid, and squeeze the coconut in cheese-cloth to extract as much moisture as possible. Discard the squeezed coconut.

Pour the coconut milk or liquid from dried coconut in a heavy saucepan, and stir in the sugar. Stir over medium heat until the sugar has dissolved. Stop stirring, and bring the liquid to a boil. Boil for 15 minutes or until the syrup forms a thread when dropped into cold water (230° F. on a candy thermometer).

Stir the shredded or grated coconut, the lime rind, and the bag of cloves into the syrup, and simmer over low heat for 15 minutes. Remove the pan from the heat; remove and discard the bag of cloves. Leave the mixture to cool.

Beat the egg yolks. Drop 4 tablespoons of the syrup from the pan into the yolks, and beat well. Stir this mixture into the syrup in the pan, and return the pan to the heat. Cook over low heat, stirring constantly, for 5 minutes or until the mixture boils and thickens.

Remove the pan from the heat and stir in the raisins, lime juice, and rum (if desired). Pour the pudding into a serving dish, and refrigerate. Serve chilled. Makes 4 servings.

**Caribbean Orange
Nut Bread**
Citrus: orange

3 cups all-purpose flour
1 tablespoon baking powder
1 teaspoon salt
¼ teaspoon ground ginger
½ teaspoon ground allspice
1 cup brown sugar
2 cups unsweetened shredded
  or flaked coconut
1 orange, juice squeezed,
  rind grated
1 egg, beaten

⅔ cup evaporated milk
1 tablespoon orange flower
  water
1 stick butter, melted
2 tablespoons chopped
  candied citrus peel (any
  kind, or a combination of
  several)
1 egg yolk, beaten with 2
  tablespoons water

Grease two 9-by-5-inch loaf pans. Preheat the oven to 350° F.
    Sift the flour, baking powder, salt, and spices into a bowl.
Beat in the sugar, coconut, grated orange rind, beaten egg,
milk, orange flower water, and melted butter. Continue beating until the dough is smooth then divide it between the two
pans. Brush the loaves with the egg yolk mixture to glaze them.
    Bake for 1 hour or until a knife inserted into the middle
of each loaf comes out clean. Cool for at least 30 minutes in
the loaf pans before turning out onto a wire rack. Makes about
20 slices.

Almond meal, which can be bought at health food stores, is made from almonds ground with or without the skins. Either kind will do for this recipe.

No-Bake Fruitcake
Citrus: lemon, orange, citron

2 cups almond meal
2 oranges, juice squeezed, rind grated
1 lemon, juice squeezed, rind grated
½ teaspoon ground cinnamon
½ teaspoon ground cloves
½ teaspoon ground allspice
¼ teaspoon ground ginger

1 cup pitted, chopped dates
1 cup mixed chopped candied citrus peel (lemon, orange, citron)
1 cup chopped pecans
1 cup golden raisins
½ cup honey
12 blanched almond halves
2 glacé cherry halves

In a large bowl mix the almond meal with the grated orange rind, spices, and dates. Rinse the chopped peel to remove excess stickiness, and dry it in absorbent paper. Add it to the mixture and stir well to combine. Stir in the chopped pecans and the raisins. Bind with the honey into a firm dough. If the mixture does not stick together, add more almond meal.

Press the mixture into a small aluminum foil loaf pan. Arrange the almond halves and cherry halves into flower shapes on top. Cover the pan with more foil and refrigerate for at least 2 days (a week is not too long). Remove from the refrigerator 2 hours before serving. Makes 8 servings.

Key Lime Pie
Citrus: lime

1¼ cups graham cracker
  crumbs
5 tablespoons sugar
¼ cup butter, softened
3 egg yolks, beaten
2 limes, rind grated, juice
  squeezed

1½ cups heavy cream
3 drops green coloring
  (optional)
2 tablespoons confectioner's
  sugar
Extra grated lime rind
  (optional)

Preheat the oven to 375° F. In a bowl combine the cracker crumbs, 2 tablespoons of the sugar, and the butter. Using a spatula or the back of a large spoon, press the crumb mixture firmly and evenly into a 9-inch pie plate. Bake 10 minutes.

In the top part of a double boiler over simmering water, combine the egg yolks, the rest of the sugar, and the lime juice. Cook, stirring constantly, until the mixture thickens, but do not let it boil. Add the grated rind. Remove from the heat and pour into a bowl. Cool to room temperature, and refrigerate for 1 hour or until thickened further.

Whip 1 cup of the cream until stiff and fold it into the lime mixture. Beat in the coloring, if desired. Pile the mixture into the pie shell and chill it for at least 8 hours or overnight.

When ready to serve, whip the remaining cream with the confectioner's sugar and pile it on top. Sprinkle with extra grated lime rind, if desired. Makes 6 to 8 servings.

Sabayon de Naranja
(Spanish
Orange Fluff)
Citrus: orange, lemon

2 tablespoons sugar
4 egg yolks
1 egg

1¼ cups milk
4 oranges, juice squeezed
½ lemon, juice squeezed

Put the sugar into the top half of a double boiler. Beat the yolks with the orange and lemon juice, and stir in the sugar. Cook over low heat, stirring constantly, until the mixture thickens enough to coat the back of a spoon. Remove the pan from the heat.

Whip the whole egg with the milk. Return the pan to the heat and, using a wire whisk, whip the egg and milk mixture into the syrup until the mixture is thick and frothy. Transfer to individual serving dishes. Serve cold. Makes 6 servings.

1 pound kumquats
1 tablespoon grated ginger
   root or ½ teaspoon
   ground ginger

4 cups sugar
4 eggs, separated
1 quart heavy cream
2 tablespoons triple sec

Kumquat Ice Cream
Citrus: kumquat

Put half the sugar into a heavy pan and add 1 cup water and the ginger. Stir until the sugar dissolves, then stop stirring and bring to a boil. Boil 5 minutes, then add the kumquats. Cover the pan and simmer the kumquats for 1 hour, stirring occasionally. Remove the pan from the heat and leave the contents to cool.

While the kumquats are cooking, heat the cream in a saucepan until it reaches the boiling point. While it is heating, beat the rest of the sugar with the egg yolks in a saucepan. Add the cream slowly to the sugar and egg yolks, stirring constantly, and cook until the mixture thickens, but do not let it boil. Remove from the heat, still stirring, and hold the base of the pan under cold water to stop the cooking process. Leave to cool to room temperature.

Stir the kumquats and any syrup they did not absorb while cooking into the cream mixture. Stir in the triple sec. Beat the egg whites into stiff peaks and fold them into the mixture. Freeze in an ice cream maker or in the freezer section of the refrigerator until firm. If using the refrigerator, beat once when half frozen to break up the crystals.

Makes 8 to 10 servings.

Orange Chess Pie
Citrus: bitter orange

These pies were originally sold by peddlers in Virginia. The word *chess* is a corruption of *cheese*, yet that ingredient soon disappeared from what were known as chess pies. The orange-flavored pie crust can be used with all sorts of other fillings. It is especially good with chocolate- and coffee-flavored cream pies.

2 cups all-purpose flour
1 teaspoon salt
1 lemon, juice squeezed,
  rind grated
1 bitter orange, rind grated,
  juice squeezed and strained
1 cup sugar

1 egg yolk
⅔ cup shortening
2 slices white bread, crusts
  removed
½ cup milk
½ cup butter
6 eggs

Grease a 9-inch pie pan. Sift the flour into a bowl with the salt, and add 2 teaspoons sugar and 1 teaspoon each of lemon and orange rind. Add the lemon juice and shortening and blend with just enough ice water to make the dough stick together, about 2 tablespoons. Roll the dough into a ball, wrap it in plastic wrap, and refrigerate it for at least 1 hour.

Preheat the oven to 350° F. Soak the bread in the milk and squeeze it to remove excess liquid. Cream the butter with the rest of the sugar and beat in the eggs. Add the bread, the orange juice, and the rest of the orange rind. Beat until the mixture is smooth. Pour it into the pie shell. Bake the pie for 45 minutes or until the crust is browned and the center firm.

Makes 8 to 10 servings.

This is the traditional southern Californian Thanksgiving dessert. Farmers used to get the eggs from their hens, the butter from their cows, and the lemons right off the tree in the yard.

Lemon Meringue Pie
Citrus: lemon

2 cups all-purpose flour
½ teaspoon salt
7 tablespoons sugar
2 lemons, juice squeezed, rind grated

3 eggs, separated
⅔ cup butter, cut into small pieces
2 tablespoons cornstarch

Sift the flour and salt with 1 tablespoon of the sugar. Add 1 teaspoon of the lemon juice, 1 egg yolk, and ½ cup butter. Mix until the dough resembles bread crumbs, then add 1 or 2 tablespoons ice water, just enough for the dough to cohere in a ball. Wrap the ball in plastic and refrigerate at least 1 hour.

Preheat the oven to 400°F. Grease a 9-inch pie plate. Roll out the dough on a floured board in a circle to fit over the bottoms and sides of the pie plate. Press the pastry firmly in the pie plate, trim the edges, and prick with a fork to release steam. Cut a sheet of aluminum foil to fit the bottom of the plate. Grease one side of the foil, and lay it greased side down over the pastry. Throw some dried beans or uncooked rice onto the foil to hold it down. Bake 15 minutes, then remove the beans and foil and bake another 5 minutes. Remove from the oven and leave the pastry to cool completely.

In a saucepan mix the cornstarch with ½ cup water. Boil 1½ cups water and pour this over the cornstarch mixture. Stir in three tablespoons of the sugar, the lemon rinds, and the juice. Cook over medium heat, stirring constantly, until the liquid boils, then simmer 2 or 3 minutes and stir in the rest of the butter. Remove the pan from the heat and beat in the two remaining egg yolks. Pour the mixture into the prepared pie shell. Make sure it touches the crust all the way around or it will shrink away while baking.

Preheat the oven to 325°F. Whip the egg whites with the rest of the sugar into stiff peaks. Pile the mixture on top of the meringue. Bake until the meringue just begins to color, about 15 minutes.

Makes 6 to 8 servings.

Orange Soufflé

Citrus: orange, lemon

4 oranges, juice squeezed,
rinds peeled
1½ cups sugar
2 tablespoons triple sec
2 tablespoons cornstarch

5 eggs, separated
2 tablespoons butter
2 tablespoons confectioner's
sugar, sifted

Slice the orange rinds in thin strips. Put them into a large pan of water and bring to a boil. Drain and rinse under cold running water. Repeat this procedure twice.

Heat 1 cup sugar with 1 cup water in a heavy-based pan, stirring until the sugar dissolves. Stop stirring, and bring the syrup to the boil. Boil 15 minutes, then add the rinds and boil 5 minutes more. Remove the pan from the heat and add the triple sec. Pour into a sauceboat and keep warm.

Strain the orange juice. Mix the juice with the cornstarch and ½ cup sugar. Heat in a saucepan, stirring constantly, until the liquid boils.

Remove the pan from the heat and beat in the butter, the egg yolks, and the grated rind. Butter a large soufflé dish, and tie a 3-inch-wide strip of wax paper around the top so it protrudes over the rim by about 1 inch. (The soufflé should rise about 1 inch above the rim of the dish, and the wax paper will keep it from spilling over.) Preheat the oven to 350° F.

Whip the egg whites into stiff peaks and fold them into the orange mixture. Pour into the soufflé dish, and bake 25 minutes or until the soufflé is well risen. Sprinkle the soufflé with the confectioner's sugar and return to the oven for 3 minutes to glaze the top. Remove the wax paper before serving. Pass the syrup separately. Makes 6 servings.

This recipe is also suitable for tangerines, tangelos, and tangors.

Caramelized Oranges
Citrus: orange

4 oranges
6 tablespoons sugar
2 tablespoons Grand Marnier

2 tablespoons slivered
almonds

Remove the rind from 2 of the oranges with a potato peeler. Peel all the oranges and put them in the freezer. Cut the rinds into very thin strips. Put them in a pan with water to cover and bring to a boil. Drain and rinse the rinds under cold water. Repeat twice.

Put the sugar in a saucepan with ½ cup water, and bring to a boil, stirring only until the sugar has dissolved. Boil 5 minutes. Add the rinds and boil another 5 minutes. Remove the rinds with a skimmer, and reserve them.

Remove the oranges from the freezer and cut off all the pith with a sharp knife, keeping the oranges in shape. Slice each orange crosswise into rings. Reassemble the rings, holding them in place with toothpicks. Put the oranges in a shallow bowl.

Pour the syrup over the oranges, spooning it over several times as it runs down and collects in the bowl. Transfer the oranges to a serving dish, and pour the syrup back into the saucepan. Cook 3 minutes or until the syrup starts to color. Quickly remove the pan from the heat, and hold the base under cold water to stop the cooking process. Add the Grand Marnier. Pour the syrup over the oranges and top them with the reserved rinds and the slivered almonds. Makes 4 servings.

**Melomakarona
(Phoenician
Honey Cookies)**
Citrus: orange, lemon

These cookies, which Greeks eat at Christmas and New Year, are said to have been introduced to Greece by the Phoenicians, who also gave Greeks the alphabet. The white wine in the recipe should be retsina, the Greek wine flavored with pine resin, but if retsina is not available, any dry white wine will do.

4 cups all-purpose flour
1 teaspoon cinnamon
½ teaspoon ground cloves
½ teaspoon ground nutmeg
¼ teaspoon salt
1 cup olive oil
¾ cup sugar

¼ cup dry white wine
1 orange, juice squeezed
2 tablespoons brandy
1 cup honey
1 lemon, juice squeezed
2 tablespoons slivered
   almonds

Sift the flour, spices, and salt into a bowl. Add 2 tablespoons of the sugar. Work the oil, wine, orange juice, and brandy into the dry ingredients until you have a fairly stiff dough. If the dough is too stiff to cohere add more orange juice or a tablespoon or two of water.

Knead the dough by hand until it is smooth and elastic, about 15 minutes. Preheat the oven to 400° F., and oil a cookie sheet. Roll pieces of the dough into balls about the size and shape of an egg. Arrange the balls of dough on the cookie sheet, pressing down to flatten them slightly. Bake for 15 minutes.

While the cookies are baking, prepare the syrup. In a heavy saucepan combine the rest of the sugar with the honey, ½ cup water, and the lemon juice. Stir only until the sugar dissolves, then boil until the liquid foams, about 5 minutes.

Remove the cookies from the oven when they are done. While they are still warm, use a ladle to dip each into the hot syrup for 2 or 3 minutes. Transfer the dipped cookies to a warmed serving platter covered with absorbent paper. Pile the cookies in a pyramid, and sprinkle them with the silvered almonds before serving. Makes about 15 cookies.

4 sugar lumps
2 large tangerines
2 tablespoons Curaçao
½ cup all-purpose flour
¼ teaspoon salt
2 eggs

1¼ cups milk
About 8 tablespoons butter
2 large tangerines, juice
  squeezed
4 tablespoons cognac

Crêpes Suzette
Citrus : tangerine

Rub two sugar lumps over the skin of one of the tangerines until the lumps turn orange. Combine the sugar with 4 tablespoons of the butter and beat until smooth. Squeeze the tangerines, and add the juice to the mixture with 1 teaspoon Curaçao. Beat until smooth.

Sift the flour and salt into a bowl. Rub the remaining sugar lumps over the other tangerine and add them to the mixture. Add the eggs, the rest of the Curaçao, and the milk, beating until smooth. Melt 2 tablespoons of the butter and add to the mixture.

When the mixture is smooth and thick, set over high heat a small skillet or crêpe pan, lightly greased with about 1 tablespoon butter. Pour a ladleful of batter into the center of the pan and cook, turning the pan so the mixture spreads. When the batter has set on one side, toss it over and cook the crêpe on the reverse side. Each side will take about 3 minutes to cook. Transfer the crêpe to a warmed platter. Repeat, lightly greasing the pan as necessary, until all the batter is used up.

Spread each crêpe with one tablespoon of the tangerine mixture. Roll up the crêpe and place it on a serving dish. When all the crêpes have been prepared in this way, warm the cognac in the crêpe pan and set it alight. Pour it over the crêpes while it is still flaming.

Makes 6 to 8 servings.

Lime Refrigerator Cheesecake
Citrus: lime

1¼ cups graham cracker crumbs
2 tablespoons butter, softened
¾ cup sugar
1 envelope unflavored gelatin
4 eggs, separated
1 cup heavy cream

2 limes, juice squeezed, rind grated
16 ounces (2 packages) cream cheese, at room temperature
¾ cup confectioner's sugar
2 tablespoons sweetened shredded coconut

Grease a 9-inch springform pan.

In a skillet combine the graham cracker crumbs with the butter and 2 tablespoons of the sugar. When the butter has melted into the crumbs and sugar, transfer the mixture to the springform pan, pressing it down with the back of a spoon so it covers the bottom of the pan and extends about a half inch up the sides. Refrigerate until needed.

In the top of a double boiler over simmering water combine the gelatin with the rest of the sugar and 3 tablespoons water. Beat the egg yolks and stir them into the gelatin mixture. Continue stirring until the gelatin has completely dissolved. Remove the pan from the heat and stir in the lime juice and the rind of 1 lime. Leave to cool. Whip ½ cup of the cream until stiff.

Beat the cream cheese until it is light and fluffy. Beat in the gelatin mixture until well blended. Stir in the remaining whipped cream.

Separately, whip the egg whites, gradually beating in ½ cup of the confectioner's sugar, until the mixture forms stiff peaks. Fold this into the cream cheese mixture.

Pile the mixture into the prepared springform pan, smoothing the top with a metal spatula. Cover the springform pan with aluminum foil and refrigerate overnight.

The next day, whip the rest of the cream with the rest of the confectioner's sugar until stiff. Put the cream into a pastry bag and pipe it around the edge of the cake. Mix the coconut with the reserved lime rind and sprinkle over the center of the cake.

Makes 10 servings.

3 small canteloupe
1 pink grapefruit
2 cups pink champagne
   or cold duck

1½ cups sugar
½ pound (1½ cups)
   strawberries, hulled and
   sliced in half lengthwise

Pink Grapefruit Sorbet

Citrus: pink grapefruit

Dissolve the sugar in 1¼ cups water over medium heat, stirring occasionally. Stop stirring and bring to a boil. Boil 5 minutes. Remove the pan from the heat and leave the syrup to cool to room temperature.

Scoop the flesh from the melons. Peel and section the grapefruit, reserving any juice and discarding as much of the skin and connective tissue as possible. In a blender or food processor purée the melon with the grapefruit. In a large bowl, combine the fruit purée with the sugar syrup and the pink champagne or cold duck. Stir in half the strawberries. Pour into the freezing trays of a refrigerator and freeze until the sorbet starts to harden. Beat to break up the crystals, and return to the refrigerator. When ready to serve, pile into glasses and decorate with the remaining strawberries. Makes 8 to 10 servings.

1 yellow grapefruit
2 large or 3 small mandarins
1 tangelo
1 tablespoon sugar
1 cup dates, pitted and
   chopped

1 cup prunes, pitted and
   halved
2 cups sweetened shredded
   coconut
½ cup pecan halves
1 cup champagne, chilled

California Ambrosia

Citrus: yellow grapefruit, mandarin, tangelo

Peel and section the citrus fruits, being careful to save the juice. Discard as much skin and connective tissue as possible. Put the sections and juice into a bowl, breaking the sections into halves or quarters with your fingers. Sprinkle with sugar and leave for 10 minutes at room temperature.

Combine the citrus with the dates, prunes, and coconut. Sprinkle with the pecans and toss lightly. Cover with plastic wrap and chill for at least 2 hours.

Divide the ambrosia into individual sundae or sherbet glasses, and sprinkle with champagne just before serving. Makes 6 to 8 servings.

Tangerine Tea Bread
Citrus: tangerine

2 sugar lumps
2 tangerines
1 envelope dried yeast
5 cups all-purpose flour
3 eggs, beaten
⅔ cup sugar
3 tablespoons oil

1 tablespoon orange flower
   water
1 egg yolk, beaten with
   2 tablespoons water
2 tablespoons sifted
   confectioner's sugar

Rub the sugar lumps over the tangerine rind until they are colored and flavored with it. Reserve the lumps. Squeeze the tangerines and warm the juice until it is hot to the touch. Pour it into a bowl, add the yeast and stir until the yeast is dissolved. Add the sugar lumps and stir till dissolved, then stir in 1 cup of the flour and mix well. Leave the mixture in a warm place, covered with a damp cloth, for about 1 hour or until doubled in bulk.

Beat the eggs with the sugar. Add the oil and orange flower water. Gradually beat in the remaining flour, then add the yeast mixture. Knead the dough for 15 minutes or until it is smooth and elastic. Grease a large bowl and put the dough into it. Cover with plastic wrap and leave in a warm place to rise until doubled in bulk, about 3 hours.

Sprinkle a baking sheet with flour. Divide the dough into 2 pieces and shape them into rounds. Place each round on the baking sheet, and flatten it slightly with your palm. Cover with a kitchen towel and leave 1 hour or until well risen.

Preheat the oven to 350° F. With a sharp knife or razor blade, make an incision all the way around each loaf just below the top. Brush the loaves with the egg yolk mixture, then sift the confectioner's sugar over them. Bake the loaves for 50 minutes or until well-browned. Leave them to cool on wire racks. Do not slice until cooled.

Makes two 8-inch loaves.

This delicious concoction is often served in Brazil as an appetizer.

Brazilian Lime Cream
Citrus: lime

2 large, very ripe avocados
4 limes

6 tablespoons confectioner's
sugar

Purée the avocado flesh in a food processor or blender. Cut one of the limes into quarters. Squeeze the juice of the other three, and strain it to eliminate seeds. Pour the juice into the avocado purée. Beat in the confectioner's sugar until the mixture is smooth.

Pile the mixture in sundae glasses and serve well chilled. Makes 4 servings.

Mandarin Mousse
Citrus: mandarin or tangelo

1 envelope unflavored gelatin
4 large mandarins or
   tangelos, rind grated,
   juice squeezed

6 eggs, separated
¾ cup sugar
1 cup heavy cream
¼ teaspoon salt

Prepare a 9-inch soufflé dish by cutting a three-inch-wide band of wax paper long enough to fit around the top. Tie it around the dish so it sticks up about 2 inches over the rim.

Stir the gelatin into 3 tablespoons of mandarin juice and leave to soften. Beat the egg yolks with ½ cup of the sugar until the mixture is pale and foaming. Beat in the rest of the juice. Transfer the mixture to the top of a double boiler. Simmer over moderate heat, stirring constantly with a wooden spoon, until the mixture coats the spoon. Do not allow it to boil.

Remove the pan from the heat and stir in the softened gelatin. Pour the mixture into a bowl and stir in the grated rind. Leave to cool. Whip the cream until it is thick but not stiff. Beat the egg whites into stiff peaks with the salt.

Fold the cream into the egg yolk mixture. Gently fold in the egg whites. Pour the mixture into the prepared soufflé dish. It should come over the rim and to the level of the wax paper. Refrigerate for at least 8 hours or overnight. Before serving, remove the wax paper. Makes 6 to 8 servings.

Old English Syllabub
Citrus: lemon

Originally, the cream was not cream but milk drawn straight from the cow into the syllabub mixture. This is a modern version, so no cow is required.

1 lemon, juice squeezed, rind peeled	2 tablespoons sugar
½ cup chablis	1¼ cups heavy cream
¼ cup applejack or whiskey	½ teaspoon grated nutmeg

Put the rind and juice of the lemon with the wine and the applejack or whiskey into a bowl. Cover and leave for 8 hours or overnight.

Strain the liquid into a deep bowl, and add the sugar. Stir until the sugar is dissolved, then pour in the cream in a very thin stream, stirring constantly, as for mayonnaise. With a wire whisk, beat the mixture until it is thick and holds a soft peak. Stir in the nutmeg.

Divide the mixture between 6 sundae or champagne glasses. Chill in the refrigerator, but serve within the hour or the mixture will separate. Makes 6 servings.

For best results in candy making you need a heavy-based preserving pan, which will distribute the heat evenly and allow the sugar to boil without burning at high temperatures. The best pans are made of solid, unlined copper and are rather expensive; stainless steel pans with copper bottoms are also good. Aluminum is unsuitable, however, since it tends to let the contents stick or burn at the very high temperatures required for candy making. You also need a candy thermometer, but this an inexpensive item. A chocolate-dipping fork is useful for dipped candies.

CANDY

Here are some other hints for successful candy making: Always preheat a thermometer in hot water before dipping it into boiling syrup. A gas oven with a pilot light is an excellent place for drying candies and candied fruits. Do not store candies in the refrigerator; they will absorb moisture from the air around them and become soggy. Keep young children out of the kitchen when making syrups; they boil at even higher temperatures than water, and when spilled on the skin they will stick to it.

2 cups brown sugar (packed)
½ cup heavy cream
½ teaspoon baking soda
1 teaspoon butter

1 orange, rind grated
½ cup pecans or walnuts,
    coarsely chopped
¼ teaspoon salt

Orange Cream Candy

Citrus: orange

Butter an 8-inch square cake pan.

In a heavy-based pan, combine the sugar with the cream and baking soda. Bring to a boil, stirring until the sugar dissolves. Boil until the syrup registers 250° F. on a candy thermometer.

Remove the pan from the heat and add the rest of the ingredients. Beat hard with a wooden spoon or spatula until the mixture thickens. Turn it out into the cake pan and spread with a metal spatula until smooth. Score it into 1-inch squares. When cold, cut the squares apart along the score marks. Store in tins lined with wax paper. Makes 1 pound.

Orange Wafers
Citrus: bitter orange

This recipe is based on a Victorian candy. It needed adapting—the original recipe recommended beating the chopped peel with the sugar for four hours! Use sweet oranges, tangerines, Temples, or tangelos if bitter oranges are not available.

24 bitter oranges, rinds peeled	About 2 pounds confectioner's sugar

Put the orange rinds into cold water and bring to a boil. Boil 5 minutes, then drain, discarding the water. Repeat this procedure twice. Drain the rinds thoroughly.

Weigh the rinds, then weigh out an equal amount of confectioner's sugar. Mince the rinds as fine as possible by hand or in a food processor. Add the sugar and beat until you have a thick paste.

Use a metal spatula to spread the paste evenly over sheets of wax paper. Leave them to dry for 4 hours in the sun or in an oven on its coolest setting. Use small cookie cutters or cocktail snack cutters to cut the wafers into fancy shapes. Remove them from the wax paper. Sprinkle them with confectioner's sugar and store them in airtight tins lined with wax paper. Makes about 2 pounds.

Orange Pecans
Citrus: orange

1½ cups sugar	1 orange, juice squeezed,
3 cups whole shelled pecans	rind grated

In a heavy-based pan, cook the sugar with the orange juice and ½ cup water, stirring until the sugar dissolves. Stop stirring and bring to a boil. Cook until the syrup registers 240° F. on a candy thermometer, between the soft- and firm-ball stages.

Remove the pan from the heat, and stir in the grated orange rind and the nuts. Keep stirring until the syrup crystallizes around the nuts. Turn the mixture out onto wax paper. When the candy is cool, break it into lumps and arrange it in paper candy cases. Store in tins lined with wax paper. Makes 1½ pounds.

2 pounds kumquats
4 tablespoons coarse salt
3 pounds (6 cups) sugar

2 cups confectioner's sugar,
sifted

Candied Kumquats

Citrus: kumquat

Slice the kumquats crosswise into three pieces, removing and discarding the seeds. Put them in a large pan of water to cover, and add the salt. Leave them for at least 24 hours at room temperature.

Drain the kumquats and rinse them under cold running water to cover by 2 inches. Put them in a large pan and add water to cover by 2 inches. Bring the water to a boil, and boil for 15 minutes or until they are tender. Drain them thoroughly, discarding the water.

Have ready 4 wire cake cooling racks or 4 sheets of wax paper. Put 1 pound of the sugar into 1 quart water and stir until the sugar dissolves. Bring to a boil without stirring. Add the kumquats and boil them a few at a time until they are transparent, removing and draining them on wire racks or wax paper as they are ready.

Leave the syrup to cool, then add the rest of the sugar. Bring to a boil again, stirring only until the sugar dissolves. Add the kumquats and boil them until the syrup registers 250°F. on a candy thermometer (the firm-ball stage).

Carefully remove the kumquats with a skimmer and lay them on wire racks to drain and cool. Sift the confectioner's sugar over them, and leave them to dry in a warm place or in an oven on the coolest setting. Place the candies in airtight containers lined with wax paper, and sprinkle confectioner's sugar over and around them. Makes about 5 pounds.

Frosted Temples or Tangelos

Citrus: Temple, tangelo

8 Temples or tangelos
2 egg whites
½ teaspoon cream of tartar

1 pound confectioner's sugar, sifted

Peel the fruits and remove any connective tissue. Thread a large, sharp needle with nylon thread. Thread the segments through the center, leaving at least ¼ inch space between them.

Beat the egg whites with the cream of tartar into stiff peaks, and beat in the sifted confectioner's sugar. Holding the ends of the thread, dip the segments into the sugar mixture, coating each very thoroughly. Stretch out the string and hang it in a warm place for the segments to dry, in the sun or under the hood of the stove. Dry for 4 to 6 hours. Store in airtight glass jars or tins lined with waxed paper. Makes about 2 pounds.

Thanks to Mrs. Thelma Nuse of Caldwell, Kansas, for this delicious recipe. Temples may be substituted for the oranges.

Orange Coconut Confection

Citrus: orange

2 oranges, juice squeezed, rind peeled
2 cups sugar
½ teaspoon salt
½ cup light corn syrup

4 cups unsweetened shredded coconut (packaged or fresh)
½ cup pecans, coarsely chopped

Put the rind in a pan with 1 quart cold water. Bring the water to a boil, then drain the rinds and discard the water. Repeat the process twice. Slice the rinds in shreds as long and thin as possible.

Put the sugar, salt, corn syrup, and orange juice in a heavy-based pan, and cook until the mixture registers 236°F. on a candy thermometer (the soft-ball stage). Add the reserved rinds, the coconut, and the pecans. Stir and remove from the heat. Drop teaspoonfuls of the mixture onto wax paper, and leave to cool. Store in airtight containers lined with wax paper. Makes about 2 pounds.

This candying method, which can also be used for citron halves and for small whole citrus fruits (prick the skins with a needle so that the syrup can penetrate thoroughly) is based on a recipe written by Nostradamus, the great French astrologer and doctor. His book, the first half of which is devoted to recipes for cosmetics and the second half to preserves and candies, was written in 1557.

Candied Citron Peel
Citrus: citron

2 large or 4 small citrons
   (about 6 pounds)
12 tablespoons coarse salt

About 6 pounds (12 cups)
   sugar

Cut the citrons in half lengthwise, then cut again lengthwise into quarters. Scoop out the central pulp and reserve it, but discard the seeds. Slice the peel into neat, thin slices. Put the tablespoons of salt. Soak for 3 days, changing the water and adding fresh salt daily.

Drain the citrons, discarding the water and pulp. Rinse the peels thoroughly in cold water to remove excess salt.

Weigh the citron peel, and weigh out an equal amount of sugar. Put the sugar in a heavy-based pan, and add 1 cup water to every pound of sugar. Bring to a boil, stirring until the sugar has dissolved. Boil for 10 minutes, then remove the pan from the heat. Let the syrup cool slightly before adding the citron peels. Leave for at least 12 hours, then boil the peels in the syrup again. Leave them to cool for 12 hours, and repeat the process once more. The citron peel should be transparent and should have absorbed most of the syrup.

Spread out the peels to dry on wire cake cooling racks or on wax paper. Leave them at room temperature, lightly covered with wax paper, until they are completely dry. This may take several weeks in a damp climate. You can speed the drying process by putting the peels in an oven at its lowest setting for 4 hours.

Makes about 6 pounds.

Candied Orange Peels

Citrus: orange

About 1½ pounds (3 cups)   6 oranges
    sugar

Squeeze the oranges, reserving the juice in a covered container in the refrigerator. Discard the seeds and connective tissue, and slice the peels into thin strips.

Soak the peels in water to cover for 24 hours at room temperature. Then put them in a pan of water to cover, and boil for 20 minutes or until tender. Drain them thoroughly, discarding the water. Slice the peels into 2-inch strips.

Mix the peels with the reserved juice, and measure the mixture. Pour it into a heavy-based pan, and add the same measure of sugar. Bring to a boil, then reduce the heat to very low. Cook, stirring frequently, until the sugar crystallizes around the orange peels. Spread the peels on plates or on wax paper to dry. Dry at room temperature, lightly covered with wax paper. The drying process may take several weeks.

Makes about 2 pounds.

Candied Grapefruit or Pomelo Peels

Citrus: grapefruit or pomelo

6 grapefruit or 4 pomelos,   About 6 cups sugar
    peeled

Slice the peels into strips about ¼ inch wide and 2 to 3 inches long. Drop them in a large bowl of cold water and soak for 12 hours or overnight.

Drain the peels and put them in a large pan of cold water to cover. Bring the water to a boil. Boil for 20 minutes or until the peels are tender.

Measure the peels, and allow 1 cup sugar to each cup peels. Put the peels in a heavy-based pan and add enough water to barely cover them. Add the sugar, and stir with a wooden spoon over medium heat until it has dissolved. Stop stirring and bring to a boil. Reduce the heat and boil slowly until the syrup is almost completely absorbed by the rinds. Pour off any surplus syrup (it is delicious with ice cream). Dip each rind in sugar. Arrange on trays covered with wax paper. Leave at room temperature for 24 hours or until dry. Store in a cool dry place in an airtight tin lined with wax paper. Makes about 3 pounds.

The original version of this candy must be stirred over heat for 4 hours or so, and is thus not very suitable for the home cook. This confection is a delicious substitute, as good as the real thing in its own way. Lime is my favorite flavor, but you can easily substitute another citrus fruit if you prefer.

Use green limes, not yellow, if you omit the coloring.

Lime Turkish Delight
Citrus: lime

3 limes, juice strained, rind grated

2 tablespoons light corn syrup

2 tablespoons (about 3 envelopes) unflavored gelatin

2 cups sugar

2 tablespoons confectioner's sugar

1 tablespoon cornstarch

3 drops green coloring (optional)

Sprinkle the insides of two or three 8-inch square cake pans or two jellyroll pans with water.

Put the sugar in a heavy-based pan and add ½ cup water. Add the rind and juice of the limes. Stir until the sugar has dissolved, then stop stirring. Add the corn syrup and bring to a boil. Reduce the heat and cook at a low boil 15 minutes.

While the syrup is boiling, stir the gelatin into ½ cup warm water. Let it soak for 10 minutes. Add it to the boiling syrup, and stir thoroughly while bringing the liquid back to a boil. Continue to stir to prevent the gelatin from forming lumps. Boil for 20 minutes. Stir in the coloring, if desired, before removing the pan from the heat.

Pour the mixture through two layers of cheesecloth into the prepared pans. Leave at room temperature for 24 hours to set.

With a sharp knife, cut the candy into 1-inch cubes. Sift the confectioner's sugar and the cornstarch together into a bowl. Roll the candy cubes in the mixture to coat them thoroughly. Place the candies in boxes lined with wax paper, and sprinkle the remaining sifted confectioner's sugar and cornstarch between them. Makes 1 pound.

Orange-flavored Candied Figs

Citrus: orange, lemon

8 ounces whole dried figs,
  or 1 pound canned figs,
  drained
2 oranges, juice squeezed,
  rind grated
1 lemon, juice squeezed,
  rind grated

1 tablespoon orange flower
  water
1 cup sugar
24 blanched almonds
½ cup mixed candied lemon
  and orange peel

Trim the hard stems from the figs. Put the juice and rind of the orange and lemon in a pan. Add the orange flower water and 3 tablespoons of the sugar, then add the figs and bring to a boil. Reduce the heat and simmer very gently until the figs are tender (from 10 to 30 minutes, depending whether they are canned or dried).

Drain the figs well (reserve the liquid for a fruit salad or another dish). Leave them to cool. Slit each fig open and stuff it with one almond and a teaspoon of candied peel. Close the opening. Roll each fig in the remaining sugar. Leave to dry overnight on wax paper before storing in airtight containers lined with wax paper. Makes about 1½ pounds.

Sweet Potato Citrus Candy

Citrus: lime, tangerine

2 pounds sweet potatoes or
  yams
2 cups confectioner's sugar,
  sifted

2 limes, juice squeezed and
  strained
2 tangerines, juice squeezed
  and strained
1 cup sugar

Boil the sweet potatoes or yams in their skins in water to cover until soft, about 30 minutes. Drain them thoroughly, then leave them to cool. When cold, peel them and mash them into a paste with the confectioner's sugar.

Put the paste in a heavy-based pan. Add the lime and tangerine juice to the paste, stirring to mix well. Cook over low heat, stirring frequently, until the juice is absorbed into the paste, about 15 minutes. Leave the paste to cool, then roll it into 1-inch balls. Roll the balls in the sugar before storing. Store in glass jars or tins lined with wax paper. Makes about 2 pounds.

Note: these candies can be dipped in chocolate if desired.

Any candied citrus rind tastes all the better for having been coated with chocolate. These candies provide the finishing touch to an elegant dinner party when served with a demitasse of strong, black coffee.

Chocolate-covered Rinds

Citrus: orange, tangelo, or Temple

3 large oranges, tangelos,
   or Temples, rind peeled
3 cups sugar

6 squares semisweet baking
   chocolate

Lay out two wire cake cooling racks or two sheets of wax paper on two large trays or on a cool work surface.

Put the rinds in a large pan and add 1 quart water. Bring to a boil, and boil 3 minutes. Drain the peels, discarding the water, and rinse them under cold running water. Put them in another quart of cold water, bring to a boil, drain, and rinse. Repeat again.

Slice the rinds as neatly as possible into strips about ¼ inch wide and 2 to 3 inches long.

Put the sugar in a heavy-based pan and add 2 cups water.

Remove the rinds from the pan. Place them on wire racks or wax paper to drain and dry for 12 hours or overnight.

Melt the chocolate in the top half of a double boiler, stirring constantly. The water in the bottom half should simmer, but it must not touch the top half of the boiler. When the chocolate has melted and is smooth, dip each piece of orange rind in it, using a dipping fork or skewer. Turn to coat the rind evenly, then transfer it immediately to a clean wire rack or to clean paper.

Do not touch the peels until the chocolate is completely hardened. Store carefully in tins or boxes lined with wax paper. Makes about ½ pound.

Old-fashioned Lemonade

Citrus: lemon, orange flower water

This recipe is from an early nineteenth-century cookbook. The orange flower water adds a subtle perfume to the drink.

8 large lemons
2 cups sugar

1 teaspoon orange flower water

Pour 1 quart water into a bowl and add the sugar. Peel the lemon rinds in thin strips and add them to the bowl. Cover and refrigerate overnight.

Squeeze the lemons and strain the juice into the bowl. Add the orange flower water. Strain again, through cheesecloth, and refrigerate for 2 hours. Serve with crushed ice. If bottled, the lemonade will keep in the refrigerator for 1 month. Makes 2½ pints.

1 cup sugar
1 quart tonic water
4 lemons

4 oranges
4 limes
2 cups crushed pineapple,
with juice

Citrus Punch
Citrus: lemon, orange, lime

Mix the sugar and tonic water with the juice of three each of the lemons, oranges, and limes. Add the crushed pineapple. Chill. Before serving, slice the remaining citrus fruits into thin rounds and use to decorate the punch. Makes 7½ cups.

4 pink grapefruit, juice
squeezed
4 oranges, juice squeezed
6 tablespoons confectioner's
sugar

½ cup cranberry juice
1 quart ginger ale
8 cherries
1 banana, sliced thin

Pink Grapefruit Cup
Citrus: grapefruit, orange

Mix the liquids and sugar, and chill. Before serving float cherries and banana slices on top. Makes 9 cups.

1 cup half-and-half
½ cup milk
1 large egg

3 tablespoons sugar
1 orange, juice squeezed
¼ teaspoon grated nutmeg

Orange Flip
Citrus: orange

In a blender combine the half-and-half, milk, egg, and sugar. While the blender is running add the orange juice and nutmeg. Serve iced. Makes 3 cups.

½ cup sugar
1 cup water
6 limes, juice squeezed

1 quart club soda
Crushed ice
8 sprigs mint

Fresh Limeade
Citrus: lime

Mix the sugar with the liquids and stir to dissolve. Put crushed ice in 8 glasses and divide the limeade between them. Decorate with the sprigs of mint. Makes 6 cups (8 servings).

Lemon Barley Water
Citrus: lemon

This traditional English drink is said to be particularly thirst quenching. It is always on hand at tennis matches to refresh the players.

9 lemons
1 cup pearl barley

2 cups sugar

Peel the lemons in thin strips, and put the peels in a large pan with the barley. Add 2 quarts water and bring to a boil. Cover and simmer for 20 minutes.

Remove the pan from the heat and leave it to cool completely. With a soup ladle remove the liquid from the top of the pan, being careful not to stir up the sediment in the bottom. When the clear liquid has been transferred to a bowl, discard the contents of the pan.

Squeeze the lemon juice and strain it through cheesecloth into the bowl. Add the sugar and stir until dissolved. When the sugar has dissolved, transfer the lemon barley water to bottles. Chill until required. Makes about 2 quarts.

Marguerita
Citrus: lime

1 lime, juice squeezed
Salt
1 jigger (1½ ounces) tequila

½ ounce (1 tablespoon)
   triple sec or Curaçao
4 tablespoons cracked ice

Rub the rims of 2 cocktail or champagne glasses with the cut half of a lime. Pour some salt into a saucer, and twirl the rims in the salt to coat them. Shake or stir the juice with the rest of the ingredients, and strain into the glasses. Makes 2 servings.

Gimlet
Citrus: lime

4 ounces (8 tablespoons)
   vodka
1 ounce (2 tablespoons)
   lime juice

1 teaspoon light corn syrup
4 tablespoons cracked ice
2 slices lime

Shake or stir the ingredients with the cracked ice, and strain into 2 chilled cocktail glasses. Decorate each glass with a slice of fresh lime. Makes 2 servings.

To make frozen daiquiris, freeze the ingredients in an ice cream maker, churning to break down the crystals as they freeze. Pulp of other fruit, such as strawberries and peaches, can be added to the mixture. Allow 2 tablespoons of pulp for the quantities listed below.

2 limes, juice squeezed
2 jiggers (3 ounces) white
   rum

2 teaspoons sugar
4 tablespoons cracked ice

Shake the ingredients vigorously in a cocktail shaker with cracked ice until the shaker frosts. Strain into 2 cocktail glasses. Makes 2 servings.

Daiquiri
Citrus: lime

4 oranges
1 cup sugar

½ cup dark rum
1 liter dry red wine

Grate the rind from the oranges, and discard it or use it in another dish. Pierce each orange with a skewer in several places, and put the oranges in a large crock. Cover them with the other ingredients. Store the crock in a cool, dark place for 3 weeks, stirring daily. Strain and bottle the liquid. Makes 1½ quarts.

Orange Wine
Citrus: orange

BIBLIOGRAPHY

Bartholomew, Elbert T., and Sinclair, Walter B. *The Lemon Fruit*, Berkeley: University of California Press, 1951.

Bonavia, Emmanuel. *The Cultivated Oranges and Lemons, etc. of India and Ceylon*. London: W. H. Allen and Company, 1888.

Cartwright, A. P. *Outspan Golden Harvest: A History of the South African Citrus Industry*. Capetown: Purnell and Sons, 1977.

Casal, U. A. *The Five Sacred Festivals of Ancient Japan*. Rutland, Vermont: Charles E. Tuttle Company, 1967.

Coit, J. Eliot. *Citrus Fruits*. New York: Macmillan Company, 1915.

Conner, Doyle, ed. *The Citrus Industry in Florida*. Bulletin No. 2. Tallahassee: Florida Department of Agriculture, 1961.

Ferrari, Iohannes Baptistae. *Hesperides sive de malorum aureorum cultura et uso libri quatuor*. Rome: Hermann Scheus, 1646.

Gallesio, Georges. *Traité du citrus*. Paris, 1811.

———. *Orange Culture: Treatise on the Citrus Family*. Translated from the French for *The Florida Agriculturalist*. Jacksonville, Florida: The Florida Agriculturalist, 1876.

Hume, Harold H. *Citrus Fruits and Their Culture*. New York: Orange Judd Company, 1904.

———. *The Cultivation of Citrus Fruits*. New York: Macmillan Company, 1926.

Isaac, Eric. "The Influence of Religion on the Spread of Citrus," *Science* 129: 179–186.

Kirkham, C. H., Jr. *The Sunkist Adventure*. Sherman Oaks, California: Sunkist Growers, 1975.

Lelong, B. M. *A Treatise on Citrus Culture in California*. Sacramento: Superintendent of State Printing, 1888.

———. *Culture of the Citrus in California*. Sacramento: Superintendent of State Printing, 1904.

Loret, Victor. "Le cédratier dans l'antiquité," *Annales de la Société Botanique de Lyon*, 1890.

Nagy, Steven, ed. *Citrus Science and Technology*. 2 vols., Westport, Connecticut: AVI Publishing Company, 1977.

Opitz, K. W., and Platt, R. G. *Citrus Growing in California*. Berkeley: University of California Cooperative Extension Service, 1969.

Reuther, Walter; Webber, Herbert John; and Batchelor, Leon Dexter. *The Citrus Industry*. 2 vols. Berkeley: University of California Press, 1973.

Risso, Antoine, and Poiteau, Antoine. *Histoire et culture des orangers*. Paris: Imprimerie de Madame Hérissant le Doux, 1818.

————. *Histoire et culture des orangers*. nouvelle edition. Paris: G. Masson and H. Plon, 1872.

Salkin, John, and Gordon, Laurie. *Orange Crate Art*. New York: Warner Books, 1976.

Sinclair, Walton B. *The Grapefruit: Its Composition, Physiology and Products*. Berkeley: University of California Division of Agricultural Science, 1972.

Sloane, Sir Hans. *A Voyage to the Islands of Madeira, Barbados, etc.* London: British Museum, 1707.

Tolkowsky, Shmuel. *Hesperides: A History of the Culture and Use of Citrus Fruits*. London: John Bale, Sons and Curnow, 1938.

————. *Peri etz hadar* [Citrus fruits, their origin and history throughout the world]. Jerusalem: Bialik Institute, 1966.

WHERE TO FIND UNUSUAL CITRUS

All the citrus-growing states have quarantine restrictions. Although seeds may be transported over state lines, most states will not allow transportation of shoots, plants, or in some cases fruit. Find out what the regulations are before buying a plant. Many nurseries will ship plants by mail order, however, providing quarantine restrictions are not being broken.

California and Florida have both established arboretums where rare citrus plants can be seen. The arboretums are fairly new, however, and at the time of writing many of the trees have not yet born fruit.

The most interesting citrus arboretum is—

The Florida Citrus Arboretum
3027 Lake Alfred Road
Winter Haven, Florida 33881
(813) 294-4267

The Florida Citrus Arboretum was started in 1975 and has almost every variety of citrus known, and some distant relatives of the citrus family such as the Bael Tree and the White Sapote.

In California, the Arboretum at California State University, Fullerton, is of even more recent origin. It features the main citrus varieties, including blood oranges and citrons, but the plants are still very young. The address is—

The Fullerton Arboretum
California State University, Fullerton
Fullerton, California 92634
(714) 773-3250

The San Gabriel Mission near Los Angeles has some of the oldest citrus trees in California, including bitter oranges, growing in the lovely mission setting. The address is—

San Gabriel Mission
537 West Mission Drive
San Gabriel, California 91776
(213) 282-5191

The following nurseries supply citrus trees, saplings, and seeds to the public. They all have stocks of unusual citrus as well as the common varieties. A few will supply by mail, but please check first. Also, remember that according to state laws mail-order plants must be free of all soil and packed in sphagnum moss, to be planted immediately upon receipt. This makes mail order a rather expensive proposition for supplier and customer alike.

California

Atkins Nursery
3129 Resche Road
Fallbrook, California 92028
(714) 728-1610

Pacific Tree Farms
4301 Lynnwood Drive
Chula Vista, California 92011
(619) 422-4200

Tropic World
26437 N Centro City Parkway
Escondido, California 92026
(619) 746-6108

Brookhall Nursery, Inc.
P.O. Box 4818
Saticoy, California 93004
(805) 647-2262

Florida

The Tree House
P.O. Box 124
Bokeelia, Florida 33922
(813) 283-1640

S. T. Brown Citrus Nursery
Route #2, Box 506
Groveland, Florida 32736
(904) 429-2368

Reed Brothers, Inc.
d/b/a Holm Citrus Seeds
505 S. Lakeshore Way
Lake Alfred, Florida 33850
(813) 956-3712

'Possum Trot Tropical Fruit
  Nursery
14955 S.W. 214th Street
Miami, Florida 33187
(305) 251-5040

Kendall Coral Reef Gardens
13100, S.W. 232nd Street
Goulds, Florida 33170
(305) 258-1035

INDEX

Continued